Psychic Healing

Psychic Healing

by
John Weldon
and
Zola Levitt

MOODY PRESS
CHICAGO

All Scripture quotations, except those noted otherwise, are from the New American Standard Bible, © 1960, 1962, 1963, 1968, 1971, 1972, 1973, 1975, and 1977 by The Lockman Foundation, and are used by permission.

Specified excerpts from Arigo: Surgeon of the Rusty Knife by John G. Fuller (Thomas Y. Crowell Company). Copyright © 1974 by John G. Fuller. Reprinted by permission of Harper & Row, Publishers, Inc. Also reprinted by permission of International Creative Management, Inc.
ISBN: 0-8024-6446-7

Acknowledgment
The authors wish to express their appreciation to the editors at Moody Press for their fine work.

2 3 4 5 6 7 Printing/LC/Year 87 86 85 84 83 82

Printed in the United States of America

Contents

CHAPTER   PAGE

Introduction   7

1. The New Medicine   13

   Man's universal interest in health. Man's move toward psychic diagnosis and psychic healing. Definitions. Public acceptance of "healers." Psychic healing and witchcraft. Psychic healing and occult-dominated society.

2. Demonic Diagnosis   29

   Psychic diagnosis. A supernatural ability. Its reality. Its appearance in primitive tribes. Its association with mesmerism and hypnotism. Its success proportional to occult involvement. Its association with medicine. Robert Leichtman. Paul Solomon. Its hostility toward God.

3. Diagnosis by Psychometry and Radionics   53

   Use of rod or pendulum to diagnose. Use of "black box" to diagnose. Why psychometry works. Cellular holography theory. Spirit intervention explanation.

4. Edgar Cayce and Psychic Diagnosis   65

   Cayce's background. Cayce's "readings." Association for Research and Enlightenment. The holistic health movement. Cayce's antibiblical views. Cayce and Christ. Health and world view. Cayce's disciple, Ross Peterson. Occultism and morality.

5. The Healers and Their Power Source   87

   Spiritistic associations. The healers—backgrounds and methods. Rolling Thun-

der. *Olga Worrall. Mr. A. Harry Edwards. Lawrence LeShan. Healers—channels for supernatural powers. Healing places—the shrines. Conclusion.*

6. **Psychic Surgery**   113
Forms of "surgery." Psychic surgery specialists. Fraud. Operating conditions. The surgeons. Josefina Sison. Arigo. Felisa Macanas. Alex Orbito and Marcelo Jainar. Juanito Flores and Jose Mercado. Juan Blance. Edivaldo. Ruthless surgical procedures. Materialization phenomena. Psychic surgery and shamanism. Spirit selection. The trance state and psychic surgery. Spirit accommodation.

7. **Spirit Powers at Work: An Analysis**   149
Unity of the spiritistic hypothesis. Semantic disguises used. Why the spirits heal. The question of fraud. Extent of the "cures." Cure rates. The faith factor. Effect of spirit healing on a population. The philosophy of occult healers.

8. **The Christian View of Psychic Healing**   191
Not harmless. Danger to the patient. Dangers to the healer. Clever counterfeits. Can be taught. Demonic activity. Occult bondage.

9. **The Biblical View of Sickness, Adversity, and Healing**   209
Positive confession. Prosperity and healing doctrines contrasted with the biblical view. Healing in the atonement. The prayer of faith. Positive sickness.

10. **Conclusion**   233
    Bibliography   237
    Index   250

Introduction

An increasing number of practitioners in the healing profession (MDs, nurses, chiropractors, etc.) are being swayed by psychic philosophies and practices, largely due to the influence of parapsychology, psychic healing, and the holistic health movements.

Patients can no longer afford the luxury of failing to determine the spiritual status of those who treat them. Failure to ascertain that may be more costly than a yearly medical bill. Practices that look entirely innocent (e.g., hand passes over the body) can become the means of occult bondage, and many spiritual healers who claim to be Christian and yielded instruments of the Holy Spirit are really psychics. Neither should one attend a "healing service" at a church without first thoroughly investigating the background of the healer. Too many psychics operate out of liberal churches. The situation is symptomatic of our times.

Numerous books on Christian healing (some found in Christian bookstores) are penned by those sympathetic to psychicism. For example, *Rediscovering the Gift of Healing* is by spiritistic sympathizer Lawrence Althouse, former President of the Spiritual Frontiers Fellowship, a group founded by medium Arthur Ford that seeks to redefine psychic abilities as spiritual gifts and otherwise integrate parapsychology and Christianity.

The last half decade has seen a variety of consequential and divisive teachings crop up within Christendom. Doctrines of world conspiracy (John Todd), sin demons, shepherding, prosperity, "Christian" psychics and "Christian" parapsychology, positive confession, healing-in-the-atonement, manifested sons of God, eastern orthodoxy, "Christian" messiahs, "passing Elijah's mantle," and a dozen others have caused no small amount of difficulty and sometimes destruction in the lives of some Christians. Many have learned the hard way. Having had one's ears tickled is small comfort when the unnecessary cost is finally admitted.

Christians should avoid those who cause division and dissension and are not according to godliness. "Now I urge you, brethren, keep your eye on those who cause dissensions and hindrances contrary to the teaching which you learned, and turn away from them" (Romans 16:17). "As a result, we are no longer to be children, tossed here and there by waves, and carried about by every wind of doctrine, by the trickery of men, by craftiness in deceitful scheming; but speaking the truth in love, we are to *grow up in all aspects* into Him, who is the head, even Christ" (Ephesians 4:14-15, italics added).

Neither has the secular world escaped. There exists today a veritable cauldron of potentially harmful practices: new disciplines, spiritistic religions, and psychological therapies. Whether it be "new" techniques and ideas in holistic health ("energy" channeling, biofeedback, yoga, applied kinesiology, acupressure, etc.), new religions (TM, est, Guru movements, Eckankar, Scientology, etc.), or the experiential and experimental psychotherapies (neo-Reichian, primal therapy, psychic music, guided imagery with music, rebirthing, sensory overload or isolation, etc.), one fact is important not to overlook: Nearly all such practices—and there are literally hundreds—have subtle and complex spiritual implications that result from the occult or humanistic world view of their originators. Most define reality and truth by experience alone. They are often designed to produce altered states of consciousness, which are then seen as validation of the teachings. Since most have an occult, humanistic, or Eastern world view, the antibiblical implications are evident. Many can develop psychic powers in the practitioners; even in the new psychotherapies, occult experiences (e.g., of the reincarnation type) are reported.[1]

Most involve the inculcation of a particular world view that insulates a person against biblical truths. Spiritual warfare has thus become much more subtle today. Many people, even Christians, have adopted such world views, hardly even recognizing them in the guise of some spiritual self-help program. Spiritual neutralization results. In the guise of spirituality, personal spiritual impotence prospers.

Parapsychology. The various forms of psychic healing constitute a subdivision of parapsychology. Despite numerous claims to the contrary, parapsychology is the scientific, and not so scientific, study of the occult. That has been well documented in a forthcoming book by Mr. Weldon.[2] The claims made by parapsychologists that they are not occultly involved are basically false. Although the methods and sometimes approach of study are different, an examination of the literature in the field, including the publications and research reports of the scientific psi laboratories, clearly show that parapsychologists study occult phenomena. For 130 years, mediumism has been the mainstay of parapsychology, even within periods of lessened interest in that particular subject.

Scientific researchers are not immune to the hazards of occult study. They may not become active occultists, although some do, and many more adopt an occult world view because of the phenomena they study. Regardless, a strictly scientific approach toward occult phenomena is insufficient protection against demonism. The judgment of God does not distinguish between scientific and nonscientific involvement with powers alien to Him. The biblical prohibitions.against the occult apply to all men. If direct or indirect contact with demonic supernaturalism defines the term *occultist*, then parapsychologists are occultists. To define them otherwise (e.g., scientific researchers of unknown natural phenomena) is to do a disservice to society. Parapsychology is opening the door wide for occultism; government, public, and media support of it should be protested, lest we reap the consequences.

Needless to say, the Christian study of parapsychology is likewise prohibited. Although several Christian parapsychological societies exist, and although far too many of the available books on "Christianity and parapsychology" *support* parapsychological research, to be a Christian parapsychologist is to be a Christian occultist, which is forbidden. If one is a Christian, one must not be a supporter of the occult.[3]

Christians today cannot afford the luxury of "spiritual" exploration. All the spiritual food needed, according to Christ, is in God's Word. Man shall live by every word that proceeds from the mouth of God (Matthew 4:4). The words He spoke are spirit and life (John 6:63). In Christ "are hidden all the treasures of wisdom and knowledge"; in Him "all the fullness of Deity dwells"; in Him we have been made complete (Colossians 2:3, 9-10). Why accept a substitute of infinitely less value?

A Christian who explores in today's jungle of alternate faiths is engaging in a form of idolatry. He is also carrying a hidden message to others. He is not merely admitting his spiritual immaturity and defeat and his disregard for the sufficiency of God and His Word—he also is telling others Christianity does not work. If Christ is the Lord, then one should serve and trust Him as Lord.

Notes

1. See *Human Behavior*, January 1977, pp. 39-40; *The Christian Parapsychologist* 3, no. 2:74; *The Brain-Mind Bulletin*, 9 March 1978; SCP (Spiritual Counterfeits Project) Journal, August 1978, p. 15; and information brochure from the Fifth International Conference of Transpersonal Psychology held in Boston, 9-14 November 1979 (sponsored by the Association for Transpersonal Psychology, Esalen Institute, and other organizations).
2. See also Clifford Wilson and John Weldon, *Occult Shock and Psychic Forces* (San Diego: Master, 1980), pp. 331-91.
3. Ibid., pp. 391-441.

1

The New Medicine

MAN'S UNIVERSAL INTEREST IN HEALTH

No one anywhere is unconcerned about his health. Man has suffered from illness since the serpent made his appearance in the Garden of Eden, and all mankind has struggled valiantly with the problem. It is supposed that in the modern world we are getting ahead of the ravages of disease. But actually our best scientific efforts have met with only limited success. Although Americans like to think they have the best of everything, this country, with its illness-prone life-style—lack of exercise, high-fat diet, excessive use of alcohol and tobacco, stressful living, and so forth—has one of the lowest overall health ratings in the industrialized world.[1] Other nations have fared little better against that common enemy.

It is popular to seek for alternative and sometimes radical solutions to modern dilemmas in politics, the family, and our very social structure. Twentieth-century man has had to devise some ingenious and unconventional ways of dealing with his unique set of problems. In the medical area, the last three decades have seen tremendous growth in the popularity of various forms of unconventional healing. Diagnosis, treatment—even "surgery"—are accomplished by "psychic" means by an ever growing sector of the population.

MAN'S MOVE TOWARD PSYCHIC DIAGNOSIS AND PSYCHIC HEALING

DEFINITIONS

Each practice—psychic diagnosis, psychic healing and psychic surgery—has a number of variations in technique.

Psychic diagnosis. Psychic diagnosis involves the clairvoyant discernment of illness apart from normal medical methods. The person may be present with the healer or on the other side of the world. The diagnosis can be made by a psychic's "seeing" into the body or the area needing treatment may be "revealed" to the healer. Diagnosis may be made by psychometry (determining the illness through an unconventional apparatus or "sensing" the problem area by touching an object belonging to the person); or diagnosis may be made by passing the hands over the body, by trance states, or by spirit guides.)

Psychic healing. The second form, psychic healing, involves the actual curing of the diagnosed ailment. This might be done by a "laying on of hands" whereby psychic energy is "injected" into the patient, or by "realigning" supposed "energy imbalances" in the body.

It is believed that a nonphysical energy system resides within each person, like the body's circulatory or nervous systems, but psychic. In the literature, it is common to find purported human energy closely linked to or part of divine energy. However, the theory teaches that when it becomes "unbalanced" or "deficient," illness often results. The psychic healer can "realign" the energy through hand passes, a form of acupressure (touching specific body areas to manipulate the energy) or other means. Whether psychic healing involves the injection of new energy or realignment of supposedly existing energy, several treatments are usually needed.

Psychic surgery. The third category, psychic surgery, involves a purported psychic opening of the body and operation upon the patient. The attending "physician" is nearly always an uneducated pagan who "operates" while in a trance state by allowing spirit doctors to work through him. Purportedly, diseased tissue, tumors, cataracts, and so on are supernaturally removed. However, as with psychic healing, several "operations" may be necessary and the ultimate healing effectiveness is dubious.

PUBLIC ACCEPTANCE OF "HEALERS"

Former astronaut Edgar Mitchell, to cite one well-known parapsychology enthusiast, is working hard to integrate psychic healing with traditional medicine. He is convinced that "psychic healers can become valuable adjuncts to hospital staffs, to general practitioners and to clinics."[2] Mitchell is most impressed with the power of psychic methodology, but he frankly indicates that it "can be as dangerous as atomic energy; in reality I think it is even more so."[3]

In Great Britain the 9,000-member World Federation of Healers (formerly the national Federation of Spiritual Healers) was recently granted government approval to treat patients in fifteen hundred hospitals throughout the country. The federation, composed largely of professed mediums, has been given corporate membership in the United Nations Association.[4]

It is interesting that a few years ago this type of healing was incorporated under the Witchcraft Act and punishable by law. Although many would claim that the general acceptance of "scientific" psychic healing is valid and helpful as a victory over superstition, we will endeavor in this book to show that psychic healing is, in fact, nothing more than a variation of common occultism. In spite of all claims, the various psychic treatments do not offer a person more hope than conventional medicine; in fact, they offer a greater chance of occult bondage than of the desired cure.

PSYCHIC HEALING AND WITCHCRAFT

Psychic healing involves a belief in man's ability to develop supernatural powers within himself through psychic forces. It borrows on various religious themes, principally reincarnation and a pantheistic or monistic view of God (that all men are part of the divine). The healing activity often involves contact with "spirit guides" and the development of trance states and other alterations of normal consciousness. The current popular *Psychic Healing Book*, by Amy Wallace* and Bill Henkin, presents such views and activities as a routine part of the psychic healer's trade.

Such activities of course line up with the traditional beliefs of occultism and witchcraft. Witches consult a "familiar" (spirit). They cultivate states of altered consciousness during their rituals. They seem to draw their powers from sources of philosophies described very much in the terms of psychic healing.

---

*Irving Wallace's daughter and coauthor of *The Book of Lists*.

Sybil Leek, one of Britain's most famous witches, indicates her beliefs in the following quotation from *None Dare Call It Witchcraft:*

> What do witches believe in? First of all, we believe that each person has the ability to develope magical powers within himself. We seek ancient wisdom through psychic forces, and know that each individual has a personal link with the Godhead. Secondly, we believe in reincarnation, the survival of the spirit after death; it is essential to our faith.[5]

Witchcraft has long been associated with psychic healing, and some covens actually specialize in it.[6] Such books as Justine Glass's *Witchcraft, the Sixth Sense* and Hans Holzer's *The Truth About Witchcraft* propose that witchcraft has a very real contribution to make to healing. And it is interesting that a certain amount of professional and public acceptance of that concept is taking place in the United States today.

Some American physicians have endorsed psychic, or mediumistic, healing, and physicians form a large part of the 1500-member *Academy of Parapsychology and Medicine*, which devotes a good deal of its time to research and psychic healing. The academy was apparently founded as the result of a dream, and its president, Robert A. Bradley, M.D., is a medium, advocating mediumism even for children.[7] He is the inventor of the sometimes criticized Bradley method of natural childbirth, an idea he claims was received from one of his spirit guides.[8] The academy's primary purpose is to integrate science and medicine with the occult.[9]

Working along similar lines in this country are the American Spiritual Healing Association and the American Healers Association. Of course their intention is purely to gather knowledge about healing.

But those aware of the biblical ramifications of traf-
fiking in the occult must recoil from such utterly
pagan and unscientific pursuits.

Elsewhere in the world, occult organizations are
mushrooming under the good name of the healing
sciences. Modern medicine seems to be taking a
step backward, in some sectors, to its primitive occultic roots. As Dr. James Fadiman, director of the
Institute of Noetic (consciousness) Sciences, states,
"The priest-shaman-doctor, which is what we started
with, is returning."[10] East meets West as the "new"
medicine from China, India, and Tibet gathers credence with the modern industrialized nations. Just a
generation ago few Americans had heard of
acupuncture, Taoist exercises, acupressure massage,
Ayurvedic healing, yoga, and the like. Today, even
the chief of Moscow's Institute of Medical Parasitology and Tropical Medicine states: "The witchdoctors
should be made a channel for the spread of modern
medical knowledge" (Los Angeles *Times*, 22
November 1979).

Of course modern people do not always turn back
to ancient times or over to the "mysterious East" for
alternative healing techniques—at least not consciously. But there are a host of new diagnostic and
treatment procedures, many of which have
Eastern-occultic roots.[11] Iridology,[12] astrologic
medicine, color and sound therapy, radionics treatments, applied kinesiology, orgonomy, biofeedback,
"past lives" therapy, reflexology or zone therapy,
rolfing, homeopathy, polarity therapy, and kirlian
photography represent just a few of the fascinatingly
named healing alternatives. They greatly vary in
validity and effectiveness, but they all represent de-
viations from the mainstream of modern medical
practice. Indeed, very few have possible medical
value.

Many people think that such remarkable techniques are merely fads among the "pop science" set. But actually, many of these new ways of healing have attracted serious scientific inquiry and, more to our point here, a renewed interest in the occult.[13]

Some qualified M.D.'s actually refer their patients to mediums and occultists for "healing" today.[14] Many branches of the medically-oriented holistic health movement are essentially occultic (see page 69).[15] The American Holistic Medical Association, the East-West Academy of Healing Arts, the Mandala Society, and the Association for Holistic Health are also representative. The dozens of conferences sponsored by the Edgar Cayce group, the Association for Research and Enlightenment (ARE.), also promote the integration of medicine and the occult.

Of course, many of those organizations and individuals do not view themselves as supporters of the occult. All these "advancements" are part of the expanding evolution of man into a higher consciousness, they believe. Most of the proponents of such movements would laugh at the idea that they are involved in the biblically prohibited rites of many an ancient society. They sincerely believe that what they have found is new and revolutionary. They hold that modern man is making great strides forward.

But the occult is not simply some kind of knowledge of the natural or spiritual realm to which only esoteric societies or sanctified devotees have access. Its true essence is more profound. All occultism sooner or later involves contact, direct or unconscious, with the demonic world, which leads to serious spiritual conflicts in any society when sufficient numbers give in to its influence and methods.

The Scriptures attest to the existence of a parallel world of invisible spirits, and it is to them that we attribute whatever success is found in psychic healing. We will be saying much more about the demon world later, but suffice it here to say that we are not surprised at the present interest in things occult. We are merely disconcerted that that interest has invaded so critical an area as medical practice.

Readers might scoff at the idea of modern America's turning to the occult for answers to medical problems. But we are doing just that, daily. The Brazilian *spiritista* hospitals, where M.D.'s and mediums work together, are beginning to reach into the United States. A hospital in Los Angeles allegedly uses Mexican witchdoctors (*curanderos*) to treat its Mexican patients.[16] A glut of books on the topic of medicine and the occult, including C. Norman Shealy's *Occult Medicine Can Save Your Life* and Stephen Brena's *Yoga and Medicine—The Merging of Yogic Concepts and Modern Medical Knowledge* (both authors are M.D.'s) are two examples of fascinating reading whose titles tell the tale.

It seems that "professional" spiritism is on the increase. Osteopath Irving Oyle's latest book, *The New American Medicine Show*, advocates spiritism, and prominent psychiatrist Gerald Jampolsky is treating terminally ill children with occult concepts prescribed in the spirit-written two-volume *Course in Miracles.*[17] Sales indicate the *course* has a following of about 100,000 students.

The famous authority on death and dying, Dr. Elizabeth Kübler-Ross, is another example of how even professionals can become occultly involved. A psychic healing advocate, she currently has about five spirit-guides ("Salem" is her favorite). Reports of sex with spirit entities at her Shantih Nilaya retreat center in California (where psychic healing and spiritism go hand in hand)[18] are less incredible than critics might imagine. In light of the religious traditions of the demonic, incubi (male demons) and succubae (female demons) are well established.[19]

Even in exceptionally scholarly works we see evidence of the trend. Editors Irving I. Zaretsky and Mark P. Leone's *Religious Movements in Contemporary America* urges the professional community to regard occultists and spiritists as actual colleagues in the healing arts.[20] Zaretsky and Leone are professors at Yale and Princeton respectively. An article by Edward J. Moody, professor at The Queens University of Belfast, Ireland, declares that satanist religions perhaps "should be encouraged" as acceptable forms of personal and societal improvement. Moody spent two and a half years as a participant observer at the First Church of Satan in San Francisco and four years involved in research of magic ritual. He discusses "the benefits of Satanism and Black Magic to the witch or magician."[21] Professor June Maclin, in "Belief, Ritual and Healing: New England Spiritualism and Mexican-American Spiritism Compared," holds that spiritistic healing restores "personal, social, and spiritual wholeness—and consequently physical health—to participants."[22]

E. Fuller Torrey, M.D., in his article "Spiritualists and Shamans as Psychotherapists," states that anthropological research along these lines "will help psychiatrists and psychologists to see spiritualists and shamans not as people who are sick and different from themselves, but rather as colleagues who are related under their respective therapeutic masks."[23]

Roger Lauer, M.D., states that mediums could prove quite useful in psychotherapeutic endeavors and that "psychic-psychiatric alliances may be quite useful, and attempts should be made to develop and assess them. . . . Mental health personnel should . . . consider professional collaboration with psychics." He tells us "a similar case could be made for the effectiveness of other types of mediumistic counseling."[24]

The *Los Angeles Times* of November 22, 1979, reported recent Russian interest in witchcraft among its African operations: "Witchdoctors should be made a channel for the spread of modern medical knowledge," stated F. F. Sopfrunov, chief of Moscow's Institute of Medical Parasitology and Tropical Medicine. A proposal was made to unite modern medicine and traditional African witchcraft.

Sociologist Laile E. Bartlett, visiting scholar at the University of California at Berkeley, stated, "Psychic healing may become commonplace someday."[25] It may indeed. Dolores Kreiger, Ph.D., R.N. (author of *The Therapeutic Touch*) has trained hundreds of nurses in her class at New York University, the largest nursing school in the US. Although she attempts to remain "scientific," her tutelage under psychic Dora Kunz and her advocacy of Eastern mystical energy concepts align her with the modern trend. In fact, she admits, "I had been taught the technique of laying on of hands by Kunz."[26]

PSYCHIC HEALING AND OCCULT-DOMINATED SOCIETY

In the ensuing chapters we will examine the psychic methods of diagnosis, healing, and surgery. We will see that each is largely dependent upon a mediumistic ability; and although the procedures are relatively new in American usage, they have been practiced for thousands of years in ancient cultures.

We will find that people are able to diagnose illness "psychically" (that is, without a normal physical examination of the patient) and then proceed to psychic healing or even psychic surgery. The last has been done throughout history, and the modern version of psychic surgery seems to be a variation of the psychic operations of the shaman, witchdoctor, or medicine man that have been practiced among primitive tribes for millennia. It is even practiced today by some gurus (e.g., Sai Baba).[27] That is not suprising, as gurus are generally occultists as well.

We will find interesting alterations of form and content in the modern versions of psychic surgery, because the spirits who control the "surgeons" accommodate their work to modern consumers. We will find that the psychic healing in general is a sobering return to primitivism, magic, and irrationalism. We will find that, far from psychic healing's representing a new age of planetary awareness, its impact is debilitating; it brings increased social and moral disintegration. It is ironic that the most technologically and scientifically advanced nation in the world is promoting among its own people a return to ancient psychicism, however unknowingly.

It is important to understand that less developed cultures are not primitive because they are historically prior. We do not take the view that men evolve in any way and that the cultures we regard as primitive are inferior to the cultures we regard as advanced. Our definition of *primitive* has to do with a society's position toward God. Some cultures are, for example, morally primitive because of their rejection of God and the resulting world view that dominates them. America, for one, has regressed into the primitive because of its relatively recent rejection of God.

Any culture that turns from God, no matter how literate or technologically advanced, will sooner or later become perverse. If that culture sinks into the abyss of occultism, the cost will be particularly severe. India, where wretched disease and starvation are a norm of daily life, is a classic example of the debilitating effect of occult practices on the national character. Attempts to get real help to such backward cultures have failed in a variety of ways, but for one common reason. Men mistakenly assume that there must be something material that will cause cultures to evolve, or advance. The culture in question is merely "historically prior," it is believed, and something can be done to bring it up to date. Then it will function as well as the "developed" cultures. That assumption is false. Although there are many variables, we could generally say that, at least in part, primitive cultures are primitive because of their rejection of God and their acceptance of the occult. Material help or material goods fail since the problem is fundamentally spiritual.

Dr. Gary North supports that view:

> Western commentators generally and correctly associate magic and primitivism. The explanation, unfortunately, tends to be environmentalistic: these societies still practice magic because they are primitive. The assumption seems to be that the West, by massive doses of foreign aid, the Peace Corps, scholarships for their bright young men to Cambridge, Oxford, or Harvard, plus free public, secular education, can bring these primitive cultures "into the twentieth century." At that point, magical practices will slowly fade away. Yet the analysis is fatally flawed. The reason why these cultures are primitive is that magic, which involves a definite world-and-life view, dominates all of them. The cultures are the product of the religion of magic, not the other way around. It is not what men possess externally that counts in the long run. What is crucial is the attitude toward God and the world that permeates the culture. By failing to recognize this fact, modern foreign-aid administrators have produced one folly after another, and this is as true of the Soviets as the

West. Primitivism is a state of mind, a set of attitudes. All attempts to overcome cultural backwardness, apart from a prior change of mind by the members of the culture in question, are doomed to failure. P. T. Bauer, a professor of economics at the London School of Economics, has written several important books on economic development, but in his 1972 study, *Dissent on Development*, he lays it on the line. The key to the economic development of a society is the character of the people. What they believe is vastly more significant than what they presently own.[28]

Societies "dominated" by the occult, be they Hinduist Indian or animist African, will not substantially improve their social, economic, and cultural conditions apart from repudiating the occult and returning to valid spirituality. (For further discussion, see North's *None Dare Call It Witchcraft* and his "Economic Commentary: Magic, Envy and Economic Underdevelopment.")[29]

If we have established that a descent into the occult is at least inadvisable, then we believe this discussion of psychic healing is important. The thousands of psychic healers operating in the Western world represent a return to aboriginal shamanism dressed in a Western cloak of respectability. This reversal comes via "science" (parapsychology, holistic health), optimistic humanism (man as god is totally self-sufficient), and in the guise of an expanse of planetary awareness (the dawning "new age"). In fact, the only new age we will get this way is one of decay and judgment. As a culture, for the sake of our descendants, we must not allow the trend toward the occult to continue.

The purpose of this book is to present the thesis that the various forms of psychic diagnosis and healing are *not* what they are purported to be by their supporters and practitioners, that is, contact with divine healing energies and/or tapping innate human psychic healing potential. These standard presentations express either a positive view (divine source) or an ethically neutral view (latent psychic healing powers). *It is our intent to present an alternate view, a negative one: Involvement with the forms of psychic healing represent to one degree or another involvement with demonism rather than with God.* Such involvement is anything but good or neutral.

NOTES

1. Harry Nelson, "American Way of Life Is Killing Us, Expert Contends," p. 1.
2. Edgar Mitchell, "New Developments in Personal Awareness," in Academy of Parapsychology and Medicine, *The Dimensions of Healing: A Symposium*, p. 8.
3. Ibid., p. 10.
4. Gilbert Anderson, "Paranormal Healing in Great Britain," in George W. Meek, ed., *Healers and the Healing Process*, p. 50.
5. *Argosy* 281 (February 1975): 75, cited in Gary K. North, *None Dare Call It Witchcraft*, p. 122.
6. Justine Glass, *Witchcraft—The Sixth Sense*, p. 123; Hans Holzer, *The Truth About Witchcraft*, pp. 172-174.
7. See Robert A. Bradley in Academy of Parapsychology and Medicine, *The Varieties of Healing Experience*, pp. 98-106.
8. Ibid.
9. Mitchell, pp. 6-7.
10. James Fadiman, "The Prime Cause of Healing," p. 16.
11. Clifford Wilson and John Weldon, *Occult Shock and Psychic Forces*, chapters 14-16.

12. A recent report of one of the first scientific studies conducted on iridology (iris diagnosis) in the US concluded that it was essentially worthless diagnostically and possibly harmful due to misdiagnosis, and that "the likelihood of correct detection was statistically no better than chance." Allie Simon, David M. Worthen, and John A. Mitas II, "An Evaluation of Iridology," p. 1385.

13. See Wilson and Weldon, *Occult Shock*, pp. 149-289, for a brief critical analysis of these methods.

14. E.g., see Antoinette May, "Meditation for Inmates," *New Realities* 1, no. 3:48.

15. Reisser and Weldon, in the forthcoming *The New Healers*, take a hard look at the old occultism in the new medicine. They not only document the occult aspects of the movement but also provide a sound alternative.

16. Leonard Nimoy, "In Search of Witchdoctors."

17. See *New Realities* 1, no. 1:9-25; 2, no. 4:48-53; 3, no. 1:54-55. For a critical analysis see *SCP* (Spiritual Counterfeits Project) *Newsletter* 7, no. 2 (June-July 1981).

18. *SCP Journal*, April 1977; *Yoga Journal*, September-October 1976, pp. 18-20. Cf. John Weldon, *Is There Life After Death?*, chapters 5-6; *Human Behavior*, September 1977, pp. 18-27.

19. Cf. Merrill F. Unger, *Demons in the World Today*, p. 32; Kurt Koch, *Christian Counseling and Occultism*, pp. 162-64.

20. Roger Lauer, "A Medium for Mental Health," in Irving I. Zaretsky and Mark P. Leone, *Religious Movements in Contemporary America*, pp. 353-54.

21. E. J. Moody, "Magical Therapy—An Anthropological Investigation of Contemporary Satanism," in Zaretsky and Leon, pp. 380-82.

22. Ibid., p. 303.

23. Ibid., p. 337.
24. Ibid., pp. 353-54.
25. Laile E. Bartlett, "New Revelations About Psychic Phenomena," p. 86.
26. Dolores Kreiger, "Therapeutic Touch and Healing Energies from Laying On of Hands," pp. 28-29. See also Shafica Karagulla, *Breakthrough to Creativity*, pp. 123-46; Dolores Kreiger, "The Potential Use of Therapeutic Touch in Healing," in Leslie J. Kaslov, ed., *Wholistic Dimensions in Healing: A Resource Guide*, pp. 182-83, 285.
27. Howard Murphett, *Sai Baba, Man of Miracles*, pp. 75-76, 159-60.
28. North, p. 174.
29. North, chapter 8, "Magic, Envy, and Foreign Aid." See Gary K. North, "Economic Commentary: Magic, Envy, and Economic Underdevelopment," *Journal of Christian Reconstruction, Symposium on Satanism*, pp. 149-62.

2

Demonic Diagnosis

Psychic Diagnosis—A Supernatural Ability

Some individuals with no medical training what-soever can diagnose physical illnesses. Sometimes they do not touch the patient. Sometimes they do not even see the patient. Part of the time they are re-markably correct in their diagnoses; sometimes they are catastrophically wrong.

Nevertheless, their work has been honored by at-tention from established medical circles. Norman C. Shealey, M.D., author of *Occult Medicine Can Save Your Life*, looks forward to the day when the American medical establishment will be utilizing the services of forty thousand psychic diagnosticians.[1]

Psychic diagnosis may be defined as the clair-voyant ability to detect physical disabilities apart from normal medical means. Although some psy-chics specialize in diagnosis, many mediums (and psychics in general) also have that amazing ability—via trance states and/or the help of "spirit guides."

Psychic diagnosis falls into two very broad categories—clairvoyance and psychometry. *Clair-*

voyance involves the psychic "seeing" into the patient's body or his aura (the supposedly etheric, nonphysical "body"). *Psychometry* involves diagnosis either by touching the patient or by touching an object belonging to the patient. In both cases, of course, there is not the vaguest clinical reason for the diagnostician's success.

ITS REALITY

There are actually as many diagnostic techniques among psychics as there are spirits who inspire them. The diagnostician may hear a voice telling him where the problems lie and what to do about them. He may diagnose illness while in a partial or full trance state, semiconscious or even fully unconscious, later remembering nothing of his analysis until told by his "conductor" (the one who placed him in the trance to begin with). Edgar Cayce (and currently Ross Peterson) was a famous psychic who worked by these means. We will analyze their work in the following chapter.

Psychometry, or extrasensory touch, seems to have no logical basis. The psychic may merely handle an object belonging to the patient. The stricken one can be thousands of miles away and the diagnosis still be reliable. Some psychics use astrology, numerology (using only names and birth dates), graphology (diagnosis from handwriting), or physiognomy (diagnosis from facial lines). The early psychics and mesmerists combined phrenology (diagnosis by head bumps) and the theories of animal magnetism to come up with diagnoses by "phrenomagnetism." Some see inside the body clairvoyantly as if they were looking at an X-ray. Autoscopy, as it is called, was also an ability of the early psychics during their "somnambulist" trances.

Others, such as Ray Stanford (a psychic who also claims to be in contact with UFOs), diagnose by the condition of the "aura." Still others simply lay hands on patients or make sweeping movements over the patients' bodies, concentrate, and receive immediate diagnoses. They may do nothing but concentrate, and still make a diagnosis of some sort. Kurt Koch, a Christian counselor and expert on occultism, mentions several examples: "For twenty years I have known of the disastrous practice of two [healers] who, without touching their patients, are able simply by concentration to diagnose with great accuracy and then prescribe homeopathic remedies."[2]

The proficient mediumship of the remarkable Ray Stanford was the impetus for the founding of the Association for the Understanding of Man in Austin, Texas, a research organization comprising Project Starlight International, which studies UFOs through technical instrumentation, and the Center for Parapsychological Research headed by Ray's brother, Rex.

In many cases an occult device is used to help the psychic develop his diagnostic abilities. Eventually he becomes proficient enough to dispense with the device entirely. Those devices include various "radionics" instruments (the "Abrams black box," pendulums, etc.), which may require some blood or a hair from the patient by which the device purportedly detects "etheric imbalances" in the patient. The use of the pendulum for diagnosis is common in Europe, and the "black box" is a pendulum-type device. Radionics instruments do not diagnose the disease itself but the supposed vibrational, or energy, imbalance causing the disease. In his books, Dr. Koch refers to several case histories, indicating some harmful consequences of pendulum diagnosis.[3]

The pendulum is used in a variety of ways. It can be held over the body, and it will begin moving when it passes over a diseased organ. It may be used to select medicine out of a medicine cabinet, or it may be hung over charts of the human body and its organs to designate problem areas. Radionics devices can be remarkably effective, but, as we will discuss later, their success ultimately rests upon the psychic powers of the operator, not the device itself.

In summary, there are several common elements to be found in occult diagnosis:

First, it is nearly always true that the psychic has no medical background; however, as some certified physicians now develop these powers, that will not be the case in the future. The current trend is moving toward more professionals (scientists, physicians, psychologists, etc.) and lay health professionals seeking to develop occult abilities.

Second, psychic power, it should be noted, is not ultimately under the control of the person using it. Along with all other occult abilities it may come and go. That is why there is still such a divergence of opinion among many scientists toward psychics like Uri Geller. Psychics cannot always "turn on" their power during scientific investigations.

Third, there is generally an occult history in the psychic person's background or family—sometimes up to four generations. That is particularly true of strong psychics.

Fourth, psychic diagnosis, despite claims to the contrary, is *not* a natural but a supernatural capacity. It lies beyond the realm of natural human potential and true science. It is not an inborn power but requires development through occult means, except when it arises from hereditary transmission. Even then it may still require development, although it may arise spontaneously in childhood or in adult life (usually the former). In essence, psychic diagnosis requires help from the "other side," as these characteristics and the frank admission of many occultists indicate.

ITS APPEARANCE IN PRIMITIVE TRIBES

Various forms of psychic diagnosis and healing have been employed throughout history. In animistic and primitive societies, where the occult flourishes, psychic diagnosis and healing are rather common and are an accepted part of the culture. Native tribes often exist in bondage to continual psychic warfare. Much of the time of the shaman (similar to a witchdoctor) is consumed in hexing the members of enemy tribes or in neutralizing death and disease hexes. Assassination magic is much more common in both primitive and modern societies than many people suspect. In fact, "death magic" is one of the more popular forms of so-called black magic. Hex-deaths do not always directly result from demonic power, although it is possible. It seems that if people believe strongly enough that they are fatally hexed, they do in fact die.

In *Hallucinogens and Shamanism*, numerous anthropologists have documented that in "primitive" witchcraft tribes, the key ingredients for "psychic diagnosis" are (1) altered states of consciousness (achieved by ritualistic music or drugs from hallucinogenic plants) and (2) contact with the spirit realm (spiritism). Associate professor of anthropology Michael Harner, who has conducted four expeditions to the Jivaro, Achuava, and Conibo-Shipibo Indians of the upper Amazon rain forest, states:

> The usual diagnosis and treatment begin with the curing shaman drinking *natemä*, tobacco juice, and *piripiri* in the late afternoon and early evening.

These drugs permit him to see into the body of the patient as though it were glass. If the illness is due to sorcery, the curing shaman will see the intruding (psychic) objects within the patient's body clearly enough to determine whether or not he can cure the sickness.[4]

Natemä is a hallucinogenic drink that promotes entry into the supernatural and spirit realms. Spirit helpers are essential to the process of shaman healing (or hexing) and are visible to the healer only by his taking the drugs.

Harner himself took the drugs and discovered a relevant fact:

For several hours after drinking the brew I found myself, although awake, in a world literally beyond my wildest dreams. I met bird-headed people, as well as dragon-like creatures who explained that they were the true gods of this world. I enlisted the services of other spirit helpers in attempting to fly through the far reaches of the Galaxy. Transported into a trance where the supernatural seemed natural, I realized that anthropologists, including myself, had profoundly underestimated the importance of the drug in affecting native ideology.[5]

Its Association with Mesmerism and Hypnotism

In more modern societies, the occurrence of psychic diagnosis correlates with revivals of interest in the occult. Our current occult revival is likely responsible for the increased prevalance of psychic diagnosis today.

Nandor Fodor, a reputable authority on psychic matters, notes some of the past occurrences and ultimate impact:

Of medical clairvoyance we find the first allusion in

Hippocrates: "The affections suffered by the body the soul sees with shut eyes." In the age of animal magnetism [mesmerism] it was widely demonstrated. The investigation committee of the French Academy of Medicine admitted, in 1831, the phenomena of medical clairvoyance. At first the gift was exercised in magnetic sleep. With the coming of spiritualism the magnetizer disappeared and both medical and ordinary clairvoyance found an outlet in spontaneous trance, or was exercised in the waking state. In the astounding psychic development of Andrew Jackson Davis [a potent medium and virulent heretic], medical clairvoyance represented the initial stage. . . . With the unfolding of spiritualism, medical clairvoyance became one of the lesser wonders. The power to diagnose was soon surpassed by the power to heal. It was thought to be less and less preposterous to employ mediums professionally for medical purposes.[6]

So we have come full circle. Psychic diagnosis helps eventually to bring about a synthesis of orthodox medicine and occult practices.

According to Norman Shealy, the first formal study of clairvoyant diagnosis began around 1847 with the British physician John Elliotson and his work with mesmerism, or "animal magnetism," as it was termed by its founder Anton Mesmer (1734-1815).[7] Actually mesmerism was the *source* for the nineteenth-century development of psychic diagnosis and was used for decades prior to Elliotson's study, in both Europe and America. In the United States at the time of Elliotson's study there was a great deal of interest in mesmerism, which culminated in the spiritist movement, begun in 1848. It is not surprising to find that Mesmer was an astrologer and mystic, or that mesmerism was the early forerunner of modern hypnosis. Modern parapsychology seems to have begun with mesmerism, which before the 1800s had become a worldwide cult.[8]

Examination of historical accounts of mesmerism discloses a very obvious tie to occultism,[9] including many spiritistic phenomena—contacting the dead in mesmeric trances, psychometry, occult personality alterations and the like, as well as astrology. In fact, the mesmerist trance is strongly linked with, if not identical to, the mediumistic trance. The term used to describe the trance state was *somnambulance*. Slater Brown, in his study of the history of spiritism, states:

> The Swedish magnetists, under the influence of their own great seer, Emanuel Swedenborg [a powerful medium], almost at once turned their attention to the invisible world and soon were receiving messages from identifiable spirits through magnetized clairvoyants. As early as 1788, sixty years before spiritualism initiated the general practice of communing with the recently deceased, a Stockholm society devoted to the study of animal magnetism reported to a sister society in France a number of cases in which somnambulists, acting as mediums, had transmitted messages from the spirit world.[10]

A well-known magnetist, J. P. F. Deleuze (author of *Practical Instruction in Animal Magnetism*, 1846), wrote to another prominent magnetist, French physician G. Billot, that "a great number of somnambulists have affirmed that they have conversed with spiritual intelligences and have been inspired and guided by them."[11] Billot stated that somnambulists had "produced flowers and other objects presumably out of thin air. . . . Some of the spirits who appeared were tangible," he said. "One not only saw but could touch them. . . . I have seen the stigmata rise on magnetized subjects, I have dispelled obsessions of evil spirits with a single word. I have seen spirits bring those material objects I told you of, and when requested make them so light that they would float."[12]

The similarity of mesmerism to mediumism here is obvious, and hence it is not surprising that the mesmerist movement both laid the basis for and was absorbed by the spiritist movement that followed it. Dr. Fodor concurs: "The conquest by spiritualism soon began and the leading Mesmerists were absorbed into the rank of the spiritualists."[13] J. P. Rindge, founder and director of the Human Dimensions Institute, also noted the parallels, many of them reminiscent of modern procedures:

> Hand passes and suggestion frequently entranced the patients, some of whom in this somnambulistic state "saw" what their physical eyes were incapable of seeing including, reportedly, their own internal organs with diagnosis (often erroneous) and prognosis (often correct) of cure. Further, many claimed to see, converse with and be healed by departed spirits. This trend mushroomed into the rapidly spreading Spiritualist movement, and was accepted by millions. It absorbed many of the Mesmerists who claimed collusion with departed spirits for the purposes of healing.[14]

One of the authoritative volumes on parapsychology says of spiritism: "No doubt its passage had been eased by the earlier conquests of the Mesmerists. The role of the trance medium fitted neatly the niche previously occupied by the somnambules, and not a few of those who began as mesmerists made the transition to Spiritualism."[15]

Mesmerism had paved the way for occult revival. There is an ominous parallel today in the great upsurge of interest in hypnotism as both an occult and a medical-diagnostic tool. Hence there is reason for concern regarding hypnotic processes in general.

There is some evidence that mesmerism and hypnotism were not altogether equivalent phenomena, but reputable thinkers are found on both sides of that question. Whatever their differences, their similarities are too clear to ignore, and wherever the exact truth lies, one fact is admitted by all: the phenomenon of mesmerism is today known as hypnotism.

The various hypnotic methods may lie within the biblically prohibited practices of "charming," "enchanting," and general magic, in the sense of the exercise of hidden or occult power over another person. In fact, the magician in ancient times (an occultist, not a performer) was described as "one who tries by certain prescribed words and actions to influence people and events, bringing about results beyond man's own power to effect."[16]

It is worth noting that Andrew Jackson Davis, an exceptionally powerful medium with an unrelenting antagonism toward Christianity, developed his powers of clairvoyant diagnosis as well as other occult powers by mesmerism, just as today hypnosis has developed a great number of mediums. Davis was known as the "John the Baptist" of the spiritist movement, and his life and teachings bear many parallels to those of Edgar Cayce, who similarily first developed his psychic diagnosis from hypnosis. Unlike Cayce, Davis, despite his prodigious occult background, became a certified medical doctor at age sixty.[17]

As suggested, the mesmeric trance is quite similar to the trance of shamans and other spiritists.[18] Even today mediums use hand (or healing) passes physically similar to the early mesmerist passes.[19] Also, the early cures by mesmerism were accompanied by demon-possession symptoms (hysterical fits, severe convulsions, etc.). Although psychological factors might also have accounted for them, they were reminiscent of the mass possessions of the Shaker community during 1837-1844,[20] and somnambulists did experience marked personality changes while in trance, as if there were another being inside them.[21] That is a common effect of "voluntary possession," such as with modern medium Jane Roberts and her spirit guide "Seth," or Arthur Ford and "Fletcher." The medium seems to become another person, or to experience direction from within.

Our interest in all this is to point out that *psychic diagnosis has long been practiced in occult circles and is in essence a spiritistic ability.* Our concern with hypnosis is that, even if it is innocuous in itself, it often results in taking people into psychic realms and experimenting with altered states of consciousness (ASC's). Those who are predisposed to the occult because of hereditary factors are particularly likely victims.[22] They may attempt to use hypnosis on, say, a medical basis, but because of their predisposition will become ensnared in the occult nonetheless. The use of a strictly neutral power does not mean that its *effects* will also be neutral. In referring to many forces of nature that are ethically neutral (chemical, gravitational, electromagnetic, etc.), Kurt Koch states:

> Yet all these forces and abilities lie within the natural sphere. It is true they can be put to either good or ill effect, but fundamentally they are neutral and natural in character. This neutral characteristic, however, is conditional and not absolute. It is forever overshadowed and influenced by two other domains.* Man is too weak to maintain his neutrality in the face of these transcendental powers. If we believe that we are masters of our gifts, then we are wrong. We are already in the hands of another power far greater than ourselves (1 Corinthians 12; Romans 12; Ephesians 2).[23]

*I.e., God or Satan

Its Success Proportional to Occult Involvement

The success of psychic diagnosis varies considerably, as one might expect. Few practitioners, if any, are 100 percent accurate although some are highly dependable—Edgar Cayce and Robert Leichtman for example. Although very few studies have been done, Norman Shealy reports from complete data on 78 patients and "at least one or more clairvoyant diagnosis carried out on almost 200. Two of the clairvoyants were 75 percent accurate and a third was 70 percent accurate in locating the site of the pain. . . . In determining the cause of the pain, the clairvoyants ranged from 65 percent accuracy down to 30 percent."[24] He also cites the 96 percent accuracy of internist Robert Leichtman. As Leichtman is a prime example of the integration of medicine and the occult, we will examine his remarkable abilities in another section.

The more accurate psychic diagnosticians are those who are reportedly in direct contact with the spirit world, and they often have a high degree of accuracy whether they see the patient himself or have only a picture—or even a name and address! (However, in the popular occult-psychic literature one hears *only* about those with high success rates. There are many more who are not so accurate.)

In some cases, success appears to be proportional to the depth of occult involvement and history. The stronger the family history in occultism, the more one opens oneself to the occult, and the longer one practices occultism, the higher the accuracy. If we look at the lives of Edgar Cayce, Olga Worrall, Robert Leichtman, and many others, that high allegiance to the occult is obvious.

ITS ASSOCIATION WITH MEDICINE

Historically medicine has had a strong link to occultism. Of course there is no necessary link between the two, but those areas over which man has little control (disease, death, the future) are by their very nature prime targets for agents involved in spiritual warfare. The dramatic activity of the demonic link to medicine in the ancient world is well chronicled in Walter A. Jayne's *The Healing Gods of Ancient Civilizations*, or the Egyptian manual "Instructions for King Merikare" (c. 2200 B.C.). Modern medicine is shot through with reminders of its occult youth. The familiar snake figure, the caduceus, is both the snake symbol of Aesculapius and a kundalini yoga symbol. The Babylonians used the Rx symbol to invoke their healing god. The doctor's prescription pad carries the eye of Horus. The Hippocratic Oath is a vow of secrecy to various deities.[25-26]

Ancient physicians often had occult associations. Hippocrates and Galen were astrologers. During the Middle Ages a physician was not qualified to practice medicine unless he was also an astrologer. Paracelsus was a virulent occultist-animist, alchemist, diviner, astrologer, and black and white magician.[27] Astrology somehow always moves in the company of modern psychic healing and occult practices such as acupuncture,[28] yogic chakras,[29] Hinduism,[30] and witchcraft.[31] Keith Thomas's *Religion and the Decline and Fall of Magic* documents the natural connections of astrology to witchcraft and many occult systems of medicine, as well as spirit contact.[32] Norman Shealy's statement, "Medicine has been occult since its very beginning—and the occult has essentially *been* medicine,"[33] is unfortunately all too accurate.

Recently there has been a relatively brief period

during which Western science has controlled medicine and healing. However, strong pressures are currently supporting the return of medicine to a more primitive heritage. For example, note Dr. Shealy's astonishing philosophy: "I sincerely believe that astrology can do a good deal to improve medical care. I feel we ought to bring this science back to the medical school, to the training of young doctors."[34]

The holistic health movement has a growing cadre of support among some politicians. Senator Edward Kennedy wrote the foreword to *Health for the Whole Person—The Complete Guide to Holistic Medicine*.[35] David Harris, president of the Association for Holistic Health, was appointed to Senator S. I. Hayakawa's advisory board on health in 1977.[36]

Actually, the idea that medicine was *originally* occult is a supposition of evolutionary thought. Medicine is supposed to have traveled, or evolved, from "primitive" (witchcraft) to "advanced" (modern technology). Biblically speaking, however, early men were more sophisticated than the secular world supposes. According to the Genesis record, man did not slowly evolve upwards from lesser creatures but was a direct creation by God, perfect in every way. Ironically, due to the Fall in the Garden, we find man spiritually degenerating, not improving, and today's man is highly inferior to the original. Thus, occult medicine (shamanism, psychic healing, witchcraft, etc.) *represents a decay from a higher state*, not an evolutionary primitivism.

ROBERT LEICHTMAN

In the 1977 *Journal of Holistic Health*, Dr. Robert Leichtman published an article titled "Clairvoyant Diagnosis—Developing Intuition and Psychic Abilities in the Diagnostic Process." The fact that he is a physician, psychic, and psychic researcher who does "extensive consultant work in psychic evaluation" for other MD's (involving thousands of patients) is indicative of both the history of medicine and the trend of the modern holistic health movement.

Dr. Leichtman walks in the best tradition of occult medicine—he admittedly receives his diagnoses from the spirit world. As one of the "New Age" representatives, he urges us to develop our psychic powers and believes his "gifts" come from God. He does not call his abilities *occult* (astrology is really "cosmobiology")—they are "intuitions" stemming from his "higher self."

Dr. Leichtman is very frank:

> If you want psychic ability turned on . . . then ask for it. . . . Talk to it [the inner oracle] and maybe it will talk back to you. Mine does. . . . There's nothing wrong with listening to voices. . . . Give your higher self a chance to communicate with you. You have got to give it permission. You have got to ask it to help. Then let it define what the answer is going to be. Let it define how it's going to present the answer to you. . . . The higher self, which is the intuitive part of you, is going to be running the show to some degree. But it's up to you to learn how to co-operate with it.[37]

Dr. Leichtman, like all nonhereditary mediums, became psychic through occult involvement. He says, "My interests led me into such things as metaphysics and occultism, and my abilities gradually began to develop."[38] In 1969, after a traditional medical background, he closed his practice and began studying metaphysics with the Unity Church. He eventually became involved with the now defunct Mind Dynamics, which finally led him into teaching courses in self-hypnosis and the development of psychic abilities.

Today, when Dr. Leichtman diagnoses he rarely sees the patient. Like Edgar Cayce, all he needs is the name, age, sex, and address of the subject. In a 1976 interview in *Psychic* magazine, he discussed his use of "spooks" (a pet name for his spirit guides):

> By that [name] I mean discarnate human beings. They're very useful. Any good psychic has several channels available as sources of information. Using one channel, I can investigate directly the field of consciousness (aura) of a subject, then draw my own conclusions. Or, I can use another channel and ask some of my spirit friends for their interpretation. (They're used to working with me, and have great knowledge of human nature.) Third, I can interview [the] spirit guides of the subject. On a complicated case, I could employ all three.[39]

Leichtman also teaches occult meditation and uses reincarnation (past lives "therapy") in his practice. His world view is that of a thoroughgoing occultist. In explaining that psychic abilities may take several lifetimes to develop, he states: "A psychic also gains experience by being someone else's spirit guide, then by working as a spirit. I know that for a fact, for I've had glimpses into some of my past lives, as well as experiences in-between as a spook. Sometimes these glimpses have been very specific in detail."[40] (Those interested in an explanation for such reincarnation experiences should consult Wilson and Weldon's *Occult Shock and Psychic Forces.*)[41]

Word of his abilities has spread fast among physicians, and he diagnoses several hundred cases a year for them. As mentioned above, his accuracy is consistently above the 90 percent level. As is typical among psychics and those who report on them, there is never any mention of the possibility of his powers arising from demons, nor any mention of the serious consequences of the occult bondage to which he is subjecting his patients. He shares the parapsychologists' well-developed ability to redefine and obscure demon activity: "Technically, I'm polarizing my consciousness on a mental plane for a while to contact the other person's field of consciousness. It means withdrawing from the physical and emotional level and using a form of telepathy."[42]

Thus we can see how Dr. Leichtman by involvement in the psychic world, involved himself in the dangerous practice of spirit contact. As is invariably the case, once he opened himself to them the spirits knew how to effectively orient him toward obedience, trust, and continuing contact. Human beings are not equipped to confront the spirit world. The cases in which naive individuals have been drawn into occult contact and bondage are legion. Generally, those people think they have made a remarkable discovery, and the full consequences of their occult practices may not be discerned, even for generations.

Dr. Leichtman explains his own "conversion" experience to the occult:

> [At first] I didn't believe in them [spirits] either. . . . But the spooks were very interested in convincing me that these things are real, because *they* were my real teachers in this whole bit and they were my teachers when it came to healing, too. What they did was to give me a whole bunch of ideas. And of course, I thought well, my mind has suddenly become brilliant. It was already great before, but now it is absolutely brilliant. I was getting all kinds of ideas from time to time and of course, the spooks said they were giving them to me, and I said uh-uh. They'd pinch me and poke me and do other things. I mean they'd pinch me hard enough to leave bruises. . . . I got kicked out of bed one morning and nobody was there. These things were very convincing.[43]

Leichtman is not alone. An ever-growing company of intelligent people is falling under these remarkable and very dangerous powers.

PAUL SOLOMON*

Former Baptist minister Paul Solomon is not a physician but a medium. He gave an intriguing lecture—"Psychic Diagnosis: Knowing Your Need by Listening to Yourself"—at the August 1978 Holistic Health Conference, sponsored by the Mandala Society and the Association for Holistic Health, in San Diego.[44] Solomon takes the view that all doctors use psychic diagnosis if they choose to really "love" their patients, because "the medium for telepathic communication is love." For him, being psychic is being "loving." He refers to the "burden" of the rational-deductive thinking process and says that the really superior way of thinking is listening to (or asking) your "higher self," or intuition.

Paul Solomon is, in essence, a trance medium like Edgar Cayce. According to *The Paul Solomon Tapes*, at the suggestion of his spirit conductor he goes into an unconscious trance state (2000 times thus far), and people ask him questions, receiving answers from what is termed "another source." Like Cayce, he remembers nothing of what occurs during the trance, and believes he is contacting the "higher self," or "higher consciousness." He claims no answer has yet been in error and that anyone can develop that ability, which the Cayce readings also recommended. Although at the conference he admitted that spirits told him to instruct his daughter in astral projection, he says "I assure you I am not a psychic."

---

*The information here is derived from Paul Solomon's statement at the August 1978 Holistic Health Conference in San Diego and from two books by him, *A Healing Consciousness* and *The Paul Solomon Tapes*.

In San Diego, Solomon actually attempted to help every member in the audience become psychic by giving instruction on psychic development. (He notes that most mystics have developed their psychic capacities via psychoses, but believes that does not have to be true in every case.)

As with Cayce, it is clear that the information coming through Solomon is not from "the higher self" but from intelligent and personal spirits transmitting information to him. Solomon admits he has given information while an EEG has shown his brain waves to be at the delta level—a state in which it is impossible to speak because the mind is so far "down." Obviously the more "down" a person is, the more control can be exerted over him.

Solomon believes that "intuition is just as valid a tool as any other process, if trained. . . . It doesn't matter where it's coming from, but if it's applicable. . . . There should not be a person in any profession not using it . . . if you're using only the rational-deductive process, you're missing a lot of answers that you ought to have."

A lack of concern with the source of clairvoyant information has made many people puppets of demons. Paradoxically, Solomon criticizes Cayce for not being more discerning about the information that came through him: "Just because information is coming from another level of mind doesn't make it valid or accurate." Yet he appears blinded to the evidence that he is doing just what Cayce did. In fact, Cayce tried to be very discerning, and, having read the Bible diligently, even suspected Satan was responsible for his "readings." However, like Solomon, he continued with them, despite their antibiblical teaching, because of their diagnostic accuracy and the "good" they were doing. (Discernment in matters like these is simply impossible apart from the Bible. Both Cayce and Solomon made themselves vulnerable to deception by rejecting its warnings about demonic deception.)

Solomon says that when we get to the point where we can put our consciousness into another person's body, then we can really do accurate diagnosis. He defines this as "consciousness projection" and not astral projection, although the latter may occur with it. In fact, there are no practical differences between the two, and they are common to many occult groups, for example, Silva Mind Control, Scientology, and so on.

Its Hostility Toward God

As related at the conference, Solomon's conversion to psychicism is a rather tragic story. After he had been a minister for years, his marriage broke up, and he turned his anger toward God. For the next five years he become involved with drinking, drugs, and sex until he reached such a point of emotional turmoil that he was near a psychotic breakdown. Instead of psychosis however, he experienced a "psychic breakthrough," which forever altered his view of God. (Such psychic transformations seem often to generate a nonbiblical world view.) Reflecting back upon that time of crisis, he stated: "I didn't pray, because God was the last thing that I wanted. But then the [old] God that I would have gone to under those circumstances is still the last thing I want."

The audience reaction at that point was, sadly, one of enthusiastic applause. It appears that within some holistic health circles there is a type of hostility toward evangelicalism. As Kurt Koch points out, occult involvement *naturally* produces obduracy against God and Christ,[45] and since many within the movement are involved in Eastern occult metaphysics, such a reaction is to be expected.

The god Solomon discovered in his psychic experience was not the God of the Bible. "It doesn't matter what you call her," he says. "Jesus was the Son of God and so are we all." God was simply some unknown "intelligent presence." Solomon's psychic experience had finalized his rejection of God. His unrepentant anger at God had opened him up to the demonic world in the guise of "an enlightening experience which bestowed upon him gifts for the betterment of mankind."

The hostility of the occult toward God and Christianity is so characteristic that Solomon's tragic testimony is not outstanding. If we look at medium Jane Roberts, we find many similar parallels. She openly displayed her animosity toward God:

> As I grew older I found it more and more difficult to accept the God of my ancestors. Irony whispered that He was as dead as they were. . . . Who wanted to sit around singing hymns to a father-God, even if He *did* exist. . . . That God, I decided, was out. I would not tolerate Him as a friend. For that matter He didn't treat His son too well either, as the story goes.[46]

As a result, through the ouija board she contacted a demon (Seth), who disguised himself as a benevolent, humorous, and advanced spirit between worldly incarnations. Her numerous "Seth books" have had wide impact. One cannot help but be reminded of Romans 1:28. "And just as they did not see fit to acknowledge God any longer, God gave them over to a depraved mind, to do those things which are not proper."

Even though spirits are too often exceptionally cunning in dealing with human psychology, their theology always betrays them. Without exception, spirit communications are antibiblical—though often religious or even partly biblical—and opposed to the true teachings of Christ. We should ask ourselves, "What then is the most logical and well-known designation for spirits who openly oppose the teaching of Christ?" They are demons.

NOTES

1. Sigrun Seutemann, "A Psychic Physician's Experiences," in George W. Meek, ed., Healers and the Healing Process, p. 95.
2. Kurt Koch, Christian Counseling and Occultism, p. 73.
3. Ibid.
4. M. J. Harner, "The Sound of Rushing Water," in Michael J. Harner, ed., Hallucinogens and Shamanism, p. 23. With permission from Natural History, June/July 1968. Copyright The American Museum of Natural History, 1968.
5. Ibid., pp. 16-17
6. Nandor Fodor, An Encyclopaedia of Psychic Science, p. 46.
7. C. Norman Shealy, "Perspectives on Psychic Diagnosis," in Meek, pp. 208-9.
8. John Beloff, "Historical Overview," in Benjamin B. Wolman, et al, eds., Handbook of Parapsychology, pp. 4-6.
9. Fodor, pp. 239-41; Slater Brown, The Heyday of Spiritualism, pp. 1-49; Jerome Eden, Animal Magnetism and the Life Energy, pp. 1-30; Jeffrey Mishlove, The Roots of Consciousness, pp. 59-64.
10. Slater Brown, p. 11.
11. Ibid.
12. Ibid., p. 12.

13. Fodor, p. 241.
14. Jeanne P. Rindge, "Perspective: An Overview of Paranormal Healing," in Meek, p. 17.
15. Beloff, p. 5.
16. J. L. Kelson, "Magician," in Merrill C. Tenney, ed., Zondervan Pictorial Encyclopedia of the Bible, 4:37.
17. Brown, chapter 7, esp. pp. 87-92. See also ARE News, July 1977.
18. Harner, p. 159; Brown, pp. 93-94.
19. H. L. Cayce, "The Varieties of Healings," in Association for Research and Enlightenment, A Symposium on the Varieties of Healing, p. 5.
20. Brown, p. 8; chapter 6, "Shakers and the Spirit World."
21. Brown, p. 3.
22. See Kurt Koch, Christian Counseling and Occultism, p. 186.
23. Kurt Koch, Demonology Past and Present, p. 56.
24. Shealy, p. 211.
25. C. Norman Shealy, Occult Medicine Can Save Your Life, preface; Walter A. Jayne, The Healing Gods of Ancient Civilizations, pp. vi, 273-75.
26. Shealy, Occult Medicine, pp. 116-17.
27. Mishlove, pp. 45-46.
28. Henry Weingarten, A Modern Introduction to Astrology, pp. 42-44.
29. George Ohsawa, Acupuncture and the Philosophy of the Far East, pp. 47-50.
30. Stephen F. Brena, Yoga and Medicine, p. 12; Alan Oken, Astrology: Evolution and Revolution, pp. 121-69.
31. Sybil Leek, My Life in Astrology.
32. Keith Thomas, Religion and the Decline of Magic, chapter 21.
33. Shealy, Occult Medicine, p. 69.
34. Ibid., p. 118.

35. Arthur Hastings, James Fadiman, and James Gordon, eds., *Health for the Whole Person— The Complete Guide to Holistic Medicine*, foreword. The book was originally prepared by the psychically oriented Institute for Noetic Sciences in San Francisco for the National Institute for Mental Health.
36. His appointment was announced at the 1977 Holistic Health Conference. See *SCP Journal*, "The Marriage of Science and Religion" (August 1978), a special issue on holistic health.
37. Robert Leichtman, "Clairvoyant Diagnosis," p. 41.
38. Robert Neubert, "Profile: Robert Leichtman, M.D.," p. 34.
39. Ibid., p. 33.
40. Ibid., p. 35.
41. Clifford Wilson and John Weldon, *Occult Shock and Psychic Forces*, chapter 9.
42. Neubert, p. 32.
43. Leichtman, p. 40.
44. Transcribed from tape by the author, who attended the conference. Cf. Paul Solomon, *The Solomon Tapes*.
45. Koch, *Christian Counseling*, p. 188.
46. Jane Roberts, *The Seth Material*, p. 6.

3

Diagnosis by Psychometry and Radionics

The assumption underlying psychometric diagnosis is that objects associated with a patient contain all the information one needs to diagnose his illness. The theory is that all matter radiates impressions and that those may be perceived by one tuned to them either "naturally" (psychically) or by means of an apparatus.

Energy rays, supposedly radiating from each of us, are said to naturally attach themselves to the objects around us. (If that were really true, however, the energy substructure of such commonly handled objects as coins should have the life history and conditions of millions of people on each one; how a psychic could pick out the most current user is the real wonder here. Yet coins are often used as psychometric devices.) Just as the water dowser claims his forked stick or dowsing rod helps to search out water or other things, the modern psychic healer may claim that a certain device or object is responsible—to one degree or another—for the diagnosis or even the healing.

Psychometry and radionics have been singled out for analysis because they are exceptionally common, often tied to research in parapsychology, advocated by some noted holistic health leaders (e.g., William Tiller), and used by some Christians.

Many "breakthroughs" in occult technology are "radionic" in nature, in the sense that a psychic person initially thinks he needs a device to operate through. The device is seen as a "breakthrough" when in reality it is a training tool later set aside. The powers do not stem from the device, but from the person.

Psychometry can be defined loosely as a clairvoyant sensitivity whereby the psychic by touching an object can pick up "impressions" (even entire scenes) of the life and experiences (including the physical condition) of the object's owner. Psychometry is a common method of psychic diagnosis. *Radionics*, or radiaesthesia, is a form of psychometry in which the healer is aided by a mechanical apparatus (dowsing rod, pendulum, "black box," etc.). Psychometry often begins with the aid of a radionics device, but the sensitive usually finds that when his psychic capacity is far enough along, the use of the device may be dispensed with entirely.

USE OF ROD OR PENDULUM TO DIAGNOSE

Diagnosis or divination by a rod or pendulum, or both, has been used for thousands of years. What is diagnosis by a pendulum? It may assume a number of forms, as can the pendulum itself. It may be swung slowly over the person's body, section by section, until the operator perceives the area of difficulty; it may be swung over a medicine cabinet to determine the appropriate medicine to be given. Even a photograph of the person or an anatomical diagram of a human body may be used to locate an illness, just as a dowser may use a pendulum or dowsing rod over a map to find water, oil, or minerals. Besides diagnosis, the rod and/or pendulum are used for scores of different purposes.

Ancient Israel was warned against dowsing in Hosea 4:12. Despite many pronouncements to the contrary, even by some Christians, we believe the use of the dowser's rod and/or pendulum is ultimately a psychic and not a natural activity; hence their use would be forbidden. Dr. Kurt Koch's books *Christian Counseling and Occultism*, *Satan's Devices*, *Between Christ and Satan*, and *The Devil's Alphabet* provide enough data to indicate clearly that a cautious attitude should be undertaken even in water dowsing. Our own perusal of dowsing literature indicates regular ties to psychic and spiritistic connections.

USE OF "BLACK BOX" TO DIAGNOSE

Virtually any object may be "diagnosed," and a large number of objects can themselves become radionic devices. The "black box" was developed by Dr. Albert Abrams, an unconventional physician. The box consisted of several variable rheostats (devices for measuring electrical currents) and a sheet of rubber mounted over a metal plate. A blood sample was placed in the box, itself connected with a metal plate attached to the forehead of a healthy person. By tapping the stomach of the healthy person and/or stroking the rubber, the "doctor" determined the illness of the patient according to the dial readings on the apparatus. After Abram's death in 1924, Dr. Ruth Drown in the United States and George de la Warr in Britain continued his work, providing some variations in technique and theory but demonstrating that the power to diagnose came from the operator, not the device. For example, Dr. Drown has made accurate diagnoses even when she has forgotten to place blood samples in the machine.[1] In other words, the operators of radionic instruments *themselves* are the "device," not the technological apparatus they use. The importance of the distinction is clear: pure occultism can become disguised by the presence of the apparatus.

WHY PSYCHOMETRY WORKS

CELLULAR HOLOGRAPHY THEORY

Lawrence Blair, author of *Rhythms of Vision*, has discussed psychometry and attempts to present it as a link between science and the occult, but he misuses science. Blair extrapolates from qualitative DNA content and cloning and makes a quantum leap to an unjustified theoretical concept of cellular holography—that each cell contains a miniature picture of the entire organism, a concept that could scientifically undergird psychometry. However, the *future potential* of DNA information, as evidenced by cloning, is hardly the same as the idea that every cell in the body is *now* equally imprinted with every other cell and condition, theoretically down to each atom.

There remain many other factors that deny a scientific basis to psychometry. How does one psychometrically pick up emotional or spiritual disorders via the supposed cellular holography? And how are psychometrists also able to foretell a person's future if we are really dealing with science here? Such questions lead us to recognize psychometric abilities as supernatural and occult, not natural and scientific.

Dr. Blair explains himself in rather incredible terms:

The envelope of energy surrounding the human body can also be detected with a pendulum, as can the Q meridians of acupuncture, in the same way that a dowser traces key lines across the country with his divining rod.

Radionics has developed this energy-detection to a finer art, and it should be stressed that it remains an art rather than a science, although producing many empirical by-products. Over the years radionics has developed a catalogue of the specific vibrationary frequencies (or "rates"), expressed in numbers, not only of the essential aetheric "radio stations" in the body—the chakras*—but also of the specific diseases which we allow to enter our system. It is not the diseases themselves, but the vibrationary imbalance underlying them which is treated. This is done with a sophisticated electronic gadget called a "radionics instrument" or "black box," which is a source of considerable hilarity among cynics—despite a surprisingly high success rate in the curing of ostensibly "incurable" diseases. This instrument both detects and treats the aetheric imbalances which give rise to a multiplicity of physical ills. In the first instance, since it is merely a form of complex pendulum, it detects malignancies from the dents, deformations or discoloration of the patient's vibrationary aura before it appears in the physical body—very much as Kirlian photography shows us a plasma or "fire body" underlying all lifeforms.

In the case of treatment, a "witness" from the patient in the form of either a hair or a drop of blood is placed in the instrument, and the dials are then set to the numerical equivalent of the required healing "rate," which is then "resonated" towards the patient regardless of his geographical distance. This choice of a hair or a drop of blood—reminiscent of witchcraft, which also requires such a sample to

---

*Supposed psychic centers integral to yogic theory and psychic enlightenment.—AUTHORS

control a subject (whether for good or ill)—may no longer be as superstitious as it sounds. Contemporary biology is aware that a single skin cell is a microcosm of the individual chemical or "vibrationary" pattern of our entire bodies, a key from which it is theoretically possible to reproduce a full-grown "clone," or twin of ourselves—which is surely a more irrational concept that witchcraft.

It is precisely this marriage between the rational and the irrational—the flat and the multidimensional—which is the vaulting-pole to visionary breakthrough. In this respect the radionics box can be seen as a twentieth century mediumistic device, an electronic "crystal ball" through which man's intuitive, as well as rational faculties are given equal rein.

Radionics is thus a further point of fusion between the spheres of science and occultism, through whose narrow connecting point can be seen the developing terrain of interior knowledge. . . .

It is significant that the fringe medicines still farthest from orthodox recognition are those which most strongly accept man's aetheric nature, yet in certain instances, such as acupuncture, they have a validity which can be scientifically demonstrated while yet being founded entirely on "mystical" precepts.[2]

SPIRIT INTERVENTION EXPLANATION

Although many people view psychometry as a natural power, Kurt Koch is convinced that it is "an occult and mediumistic ability which a number of people possess."[3] It is significant to note that one of the most influential men in radionics today, George De La Warr, claims regular help by spirits from the "other side" in his radionics research. His wife is also a medium.[4]

Dr. Koch adds a perceptive statement, which further helps to place psychometric diagnosis in its proper perspective:

The difficult question is how these psychometric powers of clairvoyance come about. Some parapsychologists, for example, Richet, Geley, Osty, Price, Gumppenberg, Gatterer, believe that clothing and in fact any object used daily by a person will become impregnated by them in some way or other. The psychometric clairvoyant is supposed to have the ability to grasp and interpret these mental-psychic impressions. This explanation is very questionable when one considers that the psychometric clairvoyant is not only able to uncover the past, but also the future of the person concerned. Here we find ourselves without doubt in the field of mediumistic fortune-telling. This deduction is confirmed when one examines the fate of such psychometrists.

In my work I have had the opportunity to examine many psychometric practices. For instance, the clairvoyant . . . wanted to come to Christ. Immediately, a state of pronounced resistance developed. Resistance to spiritual things became so strong that when trying to pray his concentration vanished entirely. Afterwards however, his mind was completely clear again. It was not even possible for him to recite a prayer, although he was an intelligent man and wanted to pray. No encouragement from the Word of God was able to penetrate this barrier. During prayer he had spells of fainting. Later I discovered that this psychometrist has also used the dangerous magic book, The 6th and 7th Book of Moses.* This would again point to the mediumistic character of psychometry, i.e., its being found in the company of black magic.[5]

The experienced Nandor Fodor adds his insight:

Many psychometrists assert that they are simply instruments and spirits do the reading. Positive proof to this effect is claimed in *Spirit Psychometry*. Trance

---

*Dr. Koch warns that even having this book in one's library can cause serious spiritual disturbances (cf. his *Between Christ and Satan*, chap. 4).—AUTHORS

mediums often ask for objects belonging to the dead to establish contact.[6]

Not all psychometrists claim spirit intervention. As with all occultism, some practitioners acknowledge their dependence on spirits, whereas others think their power comes from a personal ability, "the higher self," "universal mind," or some other man-centered concept. The key point is not that the psychometrist believes his power is not from spirits (they often purposely stay hidden, and he may not ever discover their involvement) but that those who think their powers are innate and natural perform the very same feats and produce the same phenomena as do those who utilize spirits. Hence, as with all other occultism, there are many different interpretations of what occurs but only one source. Fodor states, "The methods are individual. The percipient is passive. The exercise of the faculty requires a lax, receptive mind."[7] Psychometric diagnosis is hardly an exact science.

Perhaps one of the clearest statements of the occult, nonscientific nature of psychometry and radionics machines is found in the Theosophical Research Center's publication *The Mystery of Healing*. This discussion is worth repeating:

> Radiaesthesia is, in effect, a form of psychometry, aided by mechanical apparatus. This is not always recognized, but the fact remains that it is so. The mechanism used may be a simple divining rod, a pendulum, a complicated Abrams' "box," or one of the machines used for such work under the modern title "radiaesthesia" or "radionics". . . .
>
> It is now admitted by those who use the various types of diagnostic machines associated with radiaesthesia that for successful work it is necessary to have present a human operator of a special type. It is also well known that some operators are more

proficient than others, while in the case of certain people the machine will not work at all.*

. . . thus the mechanism used in these methods of diagnosis, whether it be a pendulum, a divining rod passed over the body, a complicated box of dials, or a photographic apparatus, is merely a means for the precise externalization of the unconscious extrasensory perceptions of the operator, whether these are accurate or not. The claim hitherto made that these machines are "a purely physical and scientific means" of diagnosis and treatment, cannot be substantiated under the present term of scientific knowledge. That they exemplify the working of certain laws of nature, still largely obscure or unrecognized, is certainly true. But no good will be done either to medical or to psychic research by denying or ignoring the psychic and psychological factors involved in their use.

Satisfactory results can be obtained without any specimen in the machine, provided the operator has knowledge of the patient's condition. See "The Chain of Life" by Dr. Guyon Richards.

Hence it follows that the accuracy or inaccuracy of diagnosis by radiaesthia will depend upon all the usual factors involved in psychic and in medical work—experience, impersonality, and the conscious or unconscious psychic capacities of the operator. . . . Since it is claimed for such treatments that "distance makes no difference," this in itself rules out any likelihood that the actual healing power is etheric or dense physical. Such a suggestion conflicts with all that is known of the laws governing the radiation of energy at the physical level. Indeed there is no known form of radiant energy that could be created by the mechanism used which could exert any appreciable influence at a distance of more than just a few yards.

---

*This is the typical parapsychologist's dilemma. Studying psychic powers requires psychics. Normal people cannot produce the phenomena needed.—AUTHORS

These criticisms do not imply that cures do not appear to take place in association with the use of these machines. What we wish to emphasize is that the diagnoses and treatments involved should be considered as psychic or extra-sensory phenomena, and that the claims made as to their being based upon purely physical science and its known laws cannot be substantiated.[8]

Now if, after all, "satisfactory results can be obtained without any specimen in the machine, provided the operator has knowledge of the patient's condition," it is exceedingly difficult to see what the machine has to do with it all. Satisfactory results are conventionally obtained, providing a physician has knowledge of the patient's condition, though admittedly the physician has to utilize the "old school" methods of prodding with a few instruments of his own.

In any case, what we seem to be involved with here is, as the above quote indicated, "psychic or extrasensory phenomena"; and we shall have to go a bit further in our investigations since the black box and so on do not surely lead us to any final conclusions.

We will do that presently. But lest the reader by this time think we are dealing with pure mumbo-jumbo and that psychic diagnosis does not really work at all, we must first pause to consider the careers of the remarkable Edgar Cayce and Ross Peterson, mediums of superb accomplishment, who give the lie to anyone who says, "What we see is what we get."

NOTES

1. *Psychic*, August 1975, p. 50.
2. Lawrence Blair, *Rhythms of Vision*, pp. 148-9. Copyright 1976 by Schocken Books. Used by permission of Schocken Books and Croom Helm Ltd., Publishers.
3. Kurt Koch, *Demonology Past and Present*, p. 125.
4. H. L. Cayce, "The Varieties of Healings," in Association for Research and Enlightenment, *A Symposium on the Varieties of Healing*, p. 5.
5. Kurt Koch, *Between Christ and Satan*, p. 47. Copyright 1962 by Kregel Publications. Used by permission.
6. Nandor Fodor, *Encyclopaedia of Psychic Science*, p. 318.
7. Ibid.
8. Theosophical Research Centre, *The Mystery of Healing*, pp. 63-65. Copyright 1958 by the Theosophical Publishing House. Used by permission.

4

Edgar Cayce and Psychic Diagnosis

The life of the amazingly successful Edgar Cayce gives us opportunity to examine the moral, theological, and spiritual effects of psychic practices upon those who indulge in them. We have indicated surprise, in view of the strangeness and lacking of objective evidence, that psychic diagnosis and the consequent healing work with any degree of success. Still we must admit that Cayce's contributions more than prove their effectiveness.

At the same time, we can gather, there are serious consequences when dealing in the occult. And what is true of psychic diagnosis is true of all areas of this arcane and biblically forbidden area.

Cayce was undoubtedly the most successful and famous of psychic diagnosticians. And Ross Peterson, claimed by some to be the "new Edgar Cayce," is presently practicing as a prominent psychic. A look at the lives of those two men will tell us a good deal about the successes and hazards of occult diagnosis and practice.

CAYCE'S BACKGROUND

If there is a modern founder of the concept of holistic health, Edgar Cayce deserves the title. Born in 1877 in Hopkinsville, Kentucky, he became one of the best-known psychic diagnosticians and healers in the country—with no medical studies whatever.

According to the standard biographies on Cayce (Joseph Millard's *Edgar Cayce: Mystery Man of Miracles*, Jess Stearn's *Edgar Cayce: The Sleeping Prophet*, Thomas Sugrue's *There Is a River* and *Stranger in the Earth*), we note psychic involvement in Cayce's family history. That would predispose the young Cayce to occult influences that came to fruition at the early age of seven.

As a child, he played with "spirit children" and had visions of "angels." Around the age of twenty, Cayce lost his voice and for over a year could hardly speak. After every remedy, including hypnosis, was tried, a second attempt at hypnosis caused Cayce to enter a trance whereby he diagnosed his own ailment and its cure. He discovered that unless he routinely entered a trance state, he would again suffer the loss of his voice. Even though he desperately wanted to be free from this condition, his only escape was in allowing his mind to be regularly appropriated by other forces, for their purposes. The power had Cayce in its full control.

CAYCE'S "READINGS"

For forty-three years, Cayce routinely entered self-induced trance states wherein he would clairvoyantly diagnose and recommend treatment for a wide range of ailments, sometimes thousands of miles removed from his patient. During his lifetime he produced over 14,000 "readings," as they were called, on various topics. Sixty-four percent described the physical ailments of thousands of people and suggested their treatment. Nearly two-thirds of his readings dealt with health. Time and again they stressed the underlying philosophy of the modern holistic health movement—that man is a divine being and contains within himself all that may be required of him eternally. Cayce's humanistic philosophy preached optimum health based on an occult view of life.

If the 14,246 readings are broken down topically, we have an idea of the diversity of the knowledge of Cayce's sources:

8976 Physical (health)
2500 Life (reincarnation-psychological)
 799 Business
 677 Dream interpretation
 401 Mental-spiritual
 223 Land (locating oil wells, investment advice, etc.)
 130 Spiritual laws and guidance for ARE (Cayce organization) study groups
 116 Work readings—developing the ARE
  76 Buried treasure
  65 For groups studying prayer and meditation for healing
  35 Aura charts
  28 World affairs
  24 Home and marriage
  16 Jesus
  14 Spiritism
  13 Atlantis
  12 Missing persons
   6 Prehistoric Egypt
   6 Psychic sources
   6 Gynecology
   4 Psychic phenomena through the subliminal
   3 Child training
   3 Reincarnation
   3 Sleep

    2 Solar system
    1 Numerology
    1 Sunspots
    1 Mayan civilization[1]

The Cayce medical files alone contain advice on several hundred different disabilities: Angina pectoris, bursitis, general cancer, deafness, epilepsy, glaucoma, hypothyroid, inguinal hernia, kidney infections, leukemia, meningitis, and so on.

Although Cayce often diagnosed correctly,, and his cures often worked, one should be cautious in accepting his methods. He was known on rare occasions to prescribe belladonna (a deadly poison) and heroin.[2] He advocated burying straws to remove warts and the placing of carbonized frog brains on the skin of a cobra victim. (Here we seem to have the possibility of direct spiritistic workings; there is certainly no physical basis for those incredible treatments, yet they were effective.)

ASSOCIATION FOR RESEARCH AND ENLIGHTENMENT

Today, hundreds of doctors utilize Cayce's psychic readings in the treatment of patients who are referred to them through the Association for Research and Enlightenment (ARE), the Edgar Cayce organization at Virginia Beach. For the last decade the ARE has sponsored yearly conferences on holistic health and is one of the largest and most influential occult organizations in the country.

The ARE also sponsors a wide variety of other programs and seminars such as home-study groups throughout the country (2500 nationally), which meet to research the Cayce readings and numerous occult subjects—for example, psychic powers and reincarnation.

Purportedly, Cayce followers were instrumental in founding the Academy of Parapsychology and Medicine mentioned in chapter 1.

THE HOLISTIC HEALTH MOVEMENT

The holistic health movement operates from basically sound ideas—personal responsibility, preventive medicine, less reliance on drugs, and treating the whole person (body, soul, and spirit). There is certainly little in those precepts that would offend the American medical consumer. However, as we have also seen, the secular holistic movement has an underlying philosophy of humanism, "the new consciousness," eastern metaphysics, and in many sectors actual occultism that corrupts the initial ideals.

Our society obviously has physicians who to a greater or lesser degree are involved in the occult. Those are still few in number, and most physicians have enough to do just to keep up with the scientific medical advances of the present time. But the holistic health movement *in general* tends to attract today's American physicians with its valid concepts for the improvement of health care.

William A. McGary, M.D., a prominent speaker at many holistic health conferences, is attempting to increase the interest of the medical world in the Cayce readings. One approach is through the ARE clinic in Phoenix, Arizona, which treats patients according to the readings' advice. As of January 1977, over 20,000 people had been treated at the clinic.[3]

But in the Cayce readings, true health is tied inextricably to the nonbiblical Cayce world view, which promotes occultism and insulates people against receiving the truth of the Christian ethic. When medical treatment involves some kind of new and perhaps ultimately negative philosophy of life, it is suspect as medical treatment.

CAYCE'S ANTIBIBLICAL VIEWS

Many people believe that Cayce was a biblical Christian and that his power came from God. His readings, however, although clearly religious and sometimes quite biblical, are essentially occult. Biblical distortion can be more devastating than biblical indifference. Cayce asserted that he had read the bible from cover to cover forty-five times, but his teaching in the light of commonly accepted interpretation of Scripture is highly suspect.[4]

Cayce tended to let his remarkable experiences become the absolute for determining his doctrine, even if that doctrine opposed the Bible. Although he did have a religious upbringing and claimed to believe the Bible literally, there is reason to question the depth of his biblical understanding. There seems to be in his writings not a breath of the knowledge of biblical salvation, since Cayce believed we must perfect ourselves through many reincarnations before we are "good enough" to go to heaven.[5] The way of salvation through perfection of the saints is an unbiblical doctrine practiced by many mystics and occultists. Salvation in the Bible, of course, is not earned by good works but freely received by faith (Ephesians 2:8-9). It goes without saying that reincarnation is a thoroughly nonbiblical concept.[6]

It is certainly tempting to think that everything that appears good comes from God. Cayce saw his own works as good, and, like God surveying creation, decided that he (Cayce) had made those good works. However, Scripture states that God's enemy imitates good if that will win him a strategic battle

(2 Corinthians 11:14). At the beginning, Cayce's trance readings were theologically noncommittal, and Cayce believed he was doing a great deal of good by diagnosing and suggesting cures, which usually worked. When the readings became nonbiblical—having unscriptural implications—he still chose to trust them because of all the "good" they had done. In the end, we find that the readings serve as a strong support for humanism, occultism, and "works salvation" and that they actually keep a person from true biblical salvation.

Cayce's life illustrates the classic pattern of those caught up in demonic fascination. He was first ensnared through the "good" being done through his gift, and his philosophy had a neutral character. Once he had done enough good to become emotionally committed to his powers, it became very difficult to abandon them. Cayce then came to the test phase, when antibiblical doctrines began to enter his teachings and practices. He began to be willing to abandon all claim to legitimate Bible doctrine and, instead, to "follow his star." Finally the ultimate phase—control by the negative spirits—was accomplished. Now Cayce was being used, in his view of things, as a puppet—a double-agent, as it were, since he was known originally as a biblical teacher. In the demonic realm, control eventually reaches a point at which the individual has no will left. Even if he chooses to escape, he cannot, which is the ultimate end of anyone's opening himself to such powers. Like so many others, Cayce was unable to outsmart or stop the forces working through him.

The idea that Cayce did "good" is a matter of conjecture. The people he cured tended to adopt his views about spiritual matters—"If he could cure me when the doctors couldn't, he must have the truth about spiritual things as well." Edgar Cayce was and is the means of oppressing millions of people by his promotion of occultism and by his turning people away from the biblical Christ and toward some other kind of salvation (2 Corinthians 11:3-4). In the end he has done a great disservice, by his unwitting support of demonic causes.

Significantly, Cayce was well aware that his career represented a steady departure from what he knew to be conservative Christianity and sound biblical exegesis. He seemed to think of himself in the terms of a prodigal son departed from the truth, tempted irresistibly by the marvelous powers he possessed. He often wished to abandon his trance states but was somehow always prevented from doing so.

A chance encounter with the famed evangelist Dwight L. Moody may have got Cayce to thinking that his unorthodox views might run contrary to a sound reading of Scripture. He later suspected that "the devil might be tempting me to do his work by operating through me when I was conceited enough to think God had given me special power."[7]

He was often not aware of the text of his readings since he was in a trance state as he voiced them, but upon learning of his first reincarnation reading he exclaimed: "But what you've been telling me today, and what the readings have been saying, is foreign to all I've believed and been taught, and all I have taught others, all my life. If ever the devil was going to play a trick on me, this would be it."[8]

His devoted friend Thomas Sugrue, author of two best-selling books on Cayce, gave a sensitive explanation of the troubling conflict the psychic experienced between the majesty of his gift and the heresies that seemed to come from it:

> Edgar had been raised as an orthodox Christian; he was a Campbellite, a member of the Christian

church,* which was an offshoot of Presbyterianism. He had been taught to interpret the Bible literally, and he had for a quarter of a century been teaching a literal interpretation of it to his Sunday school classes. He and Gertrude had finally come to believe in the reliability of his clairvoyance; now that clairvoyance informed him that what he believed about God and salvation was primitive, over-simplified and in many details untrue; it assumed a more difficult spiritual path for the soul than Edgar has imagined; . . . it acted as if the gnostics [an early Christian heresy] had not been defeated by orthodoxy in the battle that raged along the Mediterranean seventeen hundred years before; it proclaimed a Christianity so long condemned that to Edgar it sounded like the liturgies of Lucifer, the articles of Confederacy of the damned. Only by its constant reference to Christ as the apex of truth and the realization of every soul did it give him comfort. This and his knowledge that the medical diagnoses had always been accurate kept him from renouncing the clairvoyance forever.[9]

CAYCE AND CHRIST

Most suspect of all is Cayce's concept of Jesus Christ. He obviously did not look at Christ as sufficient for salvation but sought a salvation by works. Although he did teach the Bible literally in some ways, he seemed not to see the forest for the trees. The Christ Cayce refers to in his readings is simply not the biblical Jesus Christ. Only the most eccentric comprehension of the Scriptures would lead a Bible student, as Cayce was, to depart from the clear teachings of biblical salvation (Romans 3-4; 9:30; Galatians 1:6-8; etc.) and embrace a religion based on his own mystical gifts. Clearly Cayce was more intrigued by what he saw among his own good works

*Disciples of Christ.

than with that which he saw in the Bible.

We have had false Christs traveling the villages of the world, gathering converts and devotees since the resurrection of the real Christ. We are warned that in the end times "many will come in My name, saying, 'I am the Christ' " (Matthew 24:5).

We do not mean to belabor Edgar Cayce's peculiar Christian doctrine beyond the scope of studying his influence in pyschic healing. But it must be regarded that many take him to be a messiah of sorts and, in extreme cases, a kind of latter-day Christ. In examining Cayce's theological statements, however, we will find him at variance with the true Christ consistently.

Sampling quotations of Cayce's on the person and mission of Jesus Christ may enlighten one as to how unorthodox his final views became:

1. "He is an ensample [sic] for man, and only as a man, for he lived only as a man. He died only as a man."[10]

2. "Christ is not a man. Jesus was the man; Christ the messenger; Christ in all ages; Jesus in one, Joshua in another . . . etc."[11]

The idea of separating the man, Jesus, and the special messenger of God, the Christ, is common to many gnostic groups—Christian Science, Science of Mind, Unity School of Christianity, Theosophy, New Thought. It is not a new idea. Recently Reverend Sun Myung Moon has come forth with the doctrine that predicts the return of Christ indeed, but not the return of Jesus of Nazareth, a mere carpenter, who for all of His brilliant teaching fell short of His mission and was crucified a failure. Cayce's idea was that Jesus was simply a man who attained Christ's sphere or ideal or level, as any one of us might do. Thus Jesus was not born "the Christ"; He had to earn, or attain to, that exalted status. We may all do the same, in Cayce's view.

The Scriptures deal clearly and harshly with this particular false doctrine:

1 John 2:22-23, "Who is the liar but the one who denies that Jesus is the Christ? This is the antichrist, the one who denies the Father and the Son. Whoever denies the Son does not have the Father."

Luke 2:11, "For today in the city of David there has been born for you a Savior, who is Christ the Lord."

Scripturally, of course, Jesus of Nazareth was *born* the Christ. He did not achieve that position by any good works, but clearly came to us miraculously as the true Christ.

Cayce believed that Jesus the man had lived previous lives and even had been Adam. In a dialogue he gives a reincarnationist answer to a rather innocent question:

Q—"When did the knowledge come to Jesus that he was to be the savior of the world?

A—"When he fell in Eden. . . . In Adam, he brought sin."[12]

The Scriptures of course describe the one and only Jesus Christ who came to earth:

Hebrews 4:15, ". . . one who has been tempted in all things as we are, yet without sin."

2 Corinthians 5:21, ". . . Him who knew no sin. . ."

Hebrews 7:26, ". . . holy, innocent, undefiled, separated from sinners. . ."

1 Peter 2:22, ". . . WHO COMMITTED NO SIN. . ."

1 John 3:5, ". . . in Him there is no sin."

Jesus Christ is the same yesterday, today, and forever (Hebrews 13:8). And His gospel admits of no reincarnational background for the Son of God.

Cayce also believed that Christ needed to be crucified, not just for the souls of the men of the world, but for His *own* salvation. "Why the need for the Son to suffer death on the cross, to offer Himself a a sacrifice?" he said. "He offered it not alone for thyself, for the world, for the souls of men, but for His own being!"[13]

Of course the above philosophy upsets the entire Christian apple cart. If Christ were Himself impure, He would not be an efficacious offering for the sins of the rest of us. But as a matter of fact, "Christ died for the ungodly. . . . While we were yet sinners, Christ died for us" (Romans 5:6, 8).

Cayce's Christology was obviously not inspired of God since his theological understanding of the godhead was shot through with his own striking views of reincarnation and of what makes for life, death, and salvation for us all. That he was concerned with the Bible is a matter of record. That he was accurate in his understanding and teaching of it is patently untrue.

HEALTH AND WORLD VIEW

The problem with healing through the occult is that it usually comes with the requirement that one embrace the occult system. With Cayce and much of the holistic health movement, good physical health has somehow become united with an invariable antibiblical belief system.[14]

In the Cayce readings, the religious philosophy was more or less gnostic, pantheistic, and occultic. In the holistic health movement, it is primarily pantheist (everything is part of the divine nature) and/or monist (there is only one divine reality in which we all participate) and occultic. Of course it must be said there is wide divergence in the holistic health movement; it cannot be limited to those particular belief systems. The underlying idea is that if you wish true health, it will be most helpful to you to follow the party line. Without exception the belief systems advocated oppose the biblical view, so that the followers are not philosophically neutral but actively antichristian. One is reminded of such Eastern disciplines as yoga, where one may practice as a novice while holding any belief system, but in order to progress to the ultimate it is necessary to finally come into the secrets of the faith and embrace them.

Cayce was passionately convinced that each human body, indeed each atom within each cell of each human body, contained its own power of spiritual healing. He advocated an overwhelming adherence to that philosophy for the best of physical health:

> The closer the body will keep to those truths and the dependence on the abilities latent within self through trust in spiritual things, the quicker will be the response in the physical body. For all healing, mental or material, is the attuning of each atom of the body, each reflex of the brain forces, to *the awareness of the divine that lies within* each atom, each cell of the body (italics added).[15]

According to Cayce, healing influences arise when we bring about those conditions that allow us to come into closer contact with the "God within us"—by "attunement," meditation, and so on. Healing is said to be really an "expansion in consciousness," and this idea places the Cayce philosophy in the midst of the modern "new consciousness" movement, which emphasizes Eastern-occult teachings through expanded consciousness. We are not dealing with normal consciousness here but rather altered consciousness—occultic, pantheist, monist, gnostic. We must finally conclude that the real purpose behind Cayce's readings is not health care but changing the world view of the patients. Health is merely the reward for following the system, as Eve's increased knowledge was her reward for tasting the forbidden fruit.

Readers skeptical of the idea that there are actually physicians proselytizing patients by means of a health care system need to note the following quotation by V. G. Birds, M.D., a domestic health physician who has integrated Cayce's concepts into his treatment of patients. Birds is active in the Edgar Cayce Foundation's cooperating doctors program.

> One of the factors we have found is that the successful use of the [Cayce recommended] castor oil stimulates discussion with the patient of some of the philosophies of the A.R.E. . . . I had one man with gastric ulcers for eight to ten years use castor oil drops, castor packs and aloe vera, and two weeks later he was saying, "Can I bring my wife and my mother and my children in, and what's this— where'd you find out about it?" He is now reading up on some of the Cayce literature and he went to the bookstore and brought me two copies of Cayce books I hadn't had yet. So he's a strong convert.[16]

The doctor makes "converts" of his patients. Surely one does not expect the everyday physician to consider his healed patient a convert of any sort. The difference lies in the occultic nature of the Cayce system. The fervor of the healed patient is attributable to the source of the powers of the healer. Or, more simply, a bargain with Satan brings temporal reward.

Note that there is room for a distinctly Christian (or nonoccultic) holistic health movement. Our controversy is with the Eastern occultic presuppositions, unjustified pragmatism, and hostility to traditional methods, which are often components of the modern secular holistic health movement.

Cayce, the noted holistic healer, supported overwhelmingly a variety of what are normally thought of as purely mediumistic and occult phenomena: contacting the dead (despite his pronouncements to the contrary); astrology; the development of occult powers; reincarnation; trance states; and the belief in invisible and scientifically inexplicable powers that rest within each human being.[17]

In reality Cayce was no less than a strong trance medium. The information coming through him was not from his unconscious (could it possibly know all the information in the readings?) or the Akashic records, as it often claimed. Cayce's abilities were simply beyond solely human potential; hence they must have originated from a nonhuman source. The hostility to Christ and Scripture displayed so clearly in his readings is sufficient evidence of the ungodly source of Cayce's information—demons, who are the source of supernaturally received antibiblical teachings.

When we examine Cayce's heavily occult childhood, supernatural abilities, anti-Christ theology, and false prophecies, we are left with no other choice.[18] The study of the man's life is a classic in the study of the subtlety of spiritual warfare (Ephesians 6:11-18). The miseries of his life, despondency of his death (weighing only sixty pounds, he was literally burned out from his readings), and the deception of his soul are an appropriate testimonial to his source—the one called a liar and murderer from the beginning (John 8:44).

CAYCE'S DISCIPLE, ROSS PETERSON

The impact of Edgar Cayce will continue for decades. Dedicated followers will rise up to take his place and carry on his work. New converts will be made by the hundreds.

Psychic Ross Peterson is Cayce's major disciple. His praise of his master approaches that of a believer's testimony of Christ.

> I found myself believing not only in his medical readings, but in all the rest of what he taught while in trance-reincarnation, the law of karma or perfect justice, the evolution of the soul, and his whole spiritual philosophy. It made sense to me. . . . But the thing about the Cayce book that struck me more than anything else, and stuck in my mind, was Cayce's own statement, time and again, that anybody could learn to do what he did, if only they applied themselves. I couldn't get this out of my head. I resolved, God being my helper, that I was going to become someone who could do what Cayce did.[19]

After years of occult studies, yoga, self-hypnosis and hard work, Ross Peterson finally became adept at totally unconscious trance states. Soon he was doing just what Cayce had done. Like many psychics, he does not like the idea of spirits speaking through him, so he chooses to believe the personality using him is "my own higher self."[20]

Peterson is not yet as powerful as Cayce was, but he is well on the way. He is also a prime example of a statement by Edgar Mitchell: "The history of parapsychology has shown us time and again that being psychically gifted does not mean that you are spiritually or ethically developed."[21] Psychics teach that the power working through the occult and parapsychology is ethically amoral and will work through an evil person for evil means (as in witchcraft and satanism) as easily as through a moral person (who naively thinks the same power can be used for good). But in fact, because the source of power is demonic, it can hardly be ethically neutral.

Cayce's difficult life and sad end was still happier

than the earthly sojourn of Ross Peterson. Peterson has lived a life of alcoholism, sexual promiscuity, and multiple divorces. He has been in court (sometimes jail) twenty-seven times, mostly on assault and battery charges. He is currently married to his seventh wife, who is also his "conductor"—the person who helps him go into trance.[22] (As with Cayce and other mediums, the person acting as the conductor must be sympathetic to the cause.)

OCCULTISM AND MORALITY

In the world of the occult there is a strong tendency toward immorality. The Peterson readings are no exception:

> One who is truly loving as Christ would let even the most henious of murderers continue to commit yet another act and would love him as much as he would love those who are seemingly graceful and spiritual in form and manners. For there is absolutely no bias, no prejudice, no distinction in Christ love. For the true Christ loves all, anything of any dimension. See?[23]

This picture of Jesus is not the picture painted in the gospels. Although He loved sinners, he taught them repeatedly to "go and sin no more." The true Christ did not evidence love for "anything of any dimension." He displayed anger at the hypocritical Pharisees and depths of discouragement at men's lack of faith. The simplistic Christ portrayed above would be delighted with the basest of us, and salvation would supposedly be a rubber-stamp matter. In actual fact, our Lord was critical, lovingly, of those who were in error. He said to the church at Ephesus, "Yet this you do have, that you hate the deeds of the Nicolaitans, which I also hate" (Revelation 2:6). (The

Greek here says that Christ hated the deeds, not the people themselves, but it is clear from Psalm 97:10 that God does not and cannot love evil).

Peterson's Christ is most lenient on divorce, and thinks of staying in a marriage where love has died as one of the worst possible sins. Even murder can be less sinful than this.[24] In fact, divorce is not even a sin when it is "inevitable."

Tackling a difficult contemporary problem, Peterson is also lenient concerning indiscriminate abortion. He sees easy abortion as always being a logical correlation to reincarnation and pre-existence theories. One must swallow a good deal of Peterson's philosophies, or those of his spirit guides, in trying to stomach his eccentric view of this issue:

> The embryo is not a human being, in the true sense, until the soul enters this vegetative being in the womb. While the physical vehicle is being created within the womb there may be from one to 201 souls hovering around the body of the mother. The time of ensoulment, when the embryo or fetus becomes a living soul, a true human being, varies greatly.
>
> The soul generally enters the body within the day after the child is delivered from the womb. But sometimes it does not enter until two or three days after the child is delivered.
>
> Sometimes a soul will enter the body and find it not to its liking and another will enter, see?
>
> If ye were to take the life of the embryo or fetus before the soul has entered the body, what would ye have taken? Merely the physical life, no different from the life of a rabbit.
>
> And what have ye denied? There is only a simple denial of the opportunity for a soul to enter that body at that point in time. But the soul is eternal and has plenty of time.
>
> Would ye feel guilty for destroying a mere recording device? For this is fundamentally what the em-

bryo or fetus is until the soul, with its memories, its experiences, its awareness, enters into that physical form.

We see no crime in expelling the embryo or fetus from the body, other than that the body of the mother is temporarily disrupted and illness might follow. But what ye term sin? We see none.

Peterson then queried: "I wondered about cases where ensoulment might take place as early as the seventh month of pregnancy and then an abortion done. Wouldn't this be the destruction of a human being? But the readings assure us that the soul is aware of the possibility that an abortion might occur and will not inhabit that body."[25]

Without going into a great many Peterson readings, we can gather that they are essentially antilife, antimorality, and opposed to that which common sense holds to be good. Easy abortions promote a cheap view of life, and reincarnation provides the alibi. In fact, the great increase in a belief in reincarnation, due to the influx of Eastern religions, has significantly increased the chances for abortions among those thousands holding the doctrine.

Peterson's views on divorce promote escapism and personal irresponsibility and solve nothing. If problems are not worked out in one marital relationship, they are simply carried into the next one, to say nothing of the increased sexual immorality among the divorced and the emotional scars on the children. The view that we are to be so loving as to overlook murder merits no comment. The father of all lies has always been the source behind psychic communications, and his trademark is apparent.

Peterson's trance readings, like Cayce's, deny the existence of a personal devil, are pantheistic, and attempt the same distinction between Jesus and the Christ.[26]

Nearly without exception psychic communications have denied the existence of Satan. We might well expect that. Camouflage allows the enemy a freer operation behind the lines.

We could use for illustration the lives and works of various psychic diagnosticians and healers. Suffice it here to have brought out the essential points in two of the most famous. In essence, the healer destroys himself and contributes to the destruction of his patients with philosophies that simply will not accommodate this earthly life.

NOTES

1. Materials from the Association for Research and Enlightenment.
2. Thomas Sugrue, *Stranger in the Earth*, p. 217; see also Thomas Sugrue, *There Is a River*, p. 166; Joseph Millard, *Edgar Cayce, Man of Miracles*, p. 113.
3. *ARE* (Association for Research and Enlightenment) *News*, June 1977.
4. See Walter R. Martin, *The Kingdom of the Cults*, and Walter R. Martin, *The New Cults* for discussion on carelessness with clearly understood Bible doctrines.
5. Sugrue, *There Is a River*, pp. 220-21.
6. John Weldon and Clifford Wilson, *Occult Shock and Psychic Forces*, chap. 9.
7. Sugrue, *There Is a River*, p. 210.
8. Ibid.
9. Sugrue, *Stranger in the Earth*, pp. 215-16.
10. Association for Research and Enlightenment, *Jesus, the Pattern and You*, p. 53.
11. Association for Research and Enlightenment, *The Early Christian Epoch*, p. 139.
12. Ibid., pp. 136-37.

13. Ibid., p. 315.
14. See Clifford Wilson and John Weldon, *Occult Shock and Psychic Forces*, chaps. 14-18, for an analysis.
15. William McGary, "The Healing Mechanism—An Adventure in Consciousness," in Association for Research and Enlightenment, *The Healing Mechanism—An Adventure in Consciousness*, p. 4.
16. V. G. Birds, "The Castor Oil Connection," ibid., p. 14.
17. See the following Association for Research and Enlightenment circulating files: *Reincarnation*, part 1, pp. 12, 28, 31, 42; *Planetary Sojourns and Astrology*, pp. 1, 4, 39, 67; *Truth*, pp. 1, 20, 30; and *The Occult*, pp. 1-3, 19, 23-25, 31.
18. James Bjornstad, *Twentieth Century Prophecy*, chapter 4; Joseph Millard, *Edgar Cayce*; Thomas Sugrue, *There Is a River*; Sugrue, *Stranger in the Earth*; H. L. Cayce and E. E. Cayce, *The Outer Limits of Edgar Cayce's Power*; and Gary North, *None Dare Call It Witchcraft*, chapter 6.
19. Alan Spraggett, *Ross Peterson, the New Edgar Cayce*, pp. 32-33.
20. Ibid., p. 9.
21. Edgar Mitchell, "New Developments in Personal Awareness," in Academy of Parapsychology and Medicine, *The Dimensions of Healing: A Symposium*, p. 10.
22. Spraggett, pp. 14-38.
23. Ibid., pp. 141-42.
24. Ibid., p. 148.
25. Ibid., pp. 149-51.
26. Ibid., pp. 138-39, 142.

5

The Healers and Their Power Source

SPIRITISTIC ASSOCIATIONS

Like psychic diagnosis, psychic healing is an occult ability, its methods lying beyond the realm of science. There are variations here as well—healing by touch, by "magnetic passes," distant healing (usually by psychometry), and so on. What has been said of psychic diagnosis can be said of psychic healing: it is common in primitive cultures, has a long history, and is predominant in times of occult revivals. It was common to the Mesmerists. The healer has little or no medical knowledge, and virtually all cultures and eras have seen various forms of psychic healing. It is not, however, always performed through people, as psychic diagnosis must be; miraculous cures have occurred through geographical locations as well. In the past, the temples of various gods were legion that claimed cures of all types.[1] A modern parallel would be the Roman Catholic healing shrines at Fatima, Lourdes, and other places around the world.

Today, there are numerous psychic healing associations around the world, for example, the American Spiritual Healing Association and the National Federation of Spiritual Healers of Great Britain. Some of the more famous psychic healers include William Branham, Kurt Trampler, and Arthur Orlop (Germany); Gordon Turner, Mary Rogers, Harry Edwards, and George Chapmen (England); "Mr. A," Henry Rucker, Rosalyn Bruyere, Lawrence LeShan, William C. Brown, Rolling Thunder, and Ambrose and Olga Worrall (US). There are others: 200,000 in Mexico, at least a million in Brazil, and on and on.[2]

Psychic healing is without doubt a mediumistic ability. That fact is acknowledged by all who have investigated the field—although it makes some uncomfortable, and they are reluctant to admit it. These latter researchers play down the spiritistic side and concentrate on the idea of the "higher self" or some other pseudonym in their attempt to get away from the supernatural and into the "scientific" or "natural." As enthusiastic humanists they would much rather see every "new" ability as an advancement of evolving man and part of the unlimited potential of human beings.

But it seems that the truth lies elsewhere. The definitive *Healers and the Healing Process* (edited by George Meek), notes that the spiritist (i.e., reliant on the spirits) associations are evident throughout. (That particular book is something of a milestone on the topic of paranormal healing. It is the analysis of ten years of research by fourteen world renowned investigators. C. Norman Shealy calls it probably "the most comprehensive collection of information by authorities in the field of alternate medicine, the healing arts, and indeed, physics" in existence.[3]) J. Rindge points out a most interesting factor in the work:

> During the past decade, as the research reported in the following chapters progressed, one very intri-

guing fact emerged. The only large concentrations of healers seem to be in countries where the belief systems involve what is generally known as Spiritualism or Spiritism.[4]

Hans Naegeli-Osjord states, "In both Brazil and the Philippines the healers have developed almost entirely in the confines of spiritualistic communities."[5] That is true of other countries as well. Whenever psychic healers are discussed, the topic of mediumism crops up. In Holzer's *Beyond Medicine*, the careers of twenty-one healers are discussed, nineteen of whom are admitted mediums.[6] It is understandable that not every healer wants to be called a medium. Most do not. Holzer comments to this effect but notes that the source of the healing power is the same, regardless of the manifestation or style.

> Psychic healing, of course, is in itself part of the occult sciences; the majority of mediums, whether professional or amateur, have some healing gift and are able to perform healings—largely because the force that makes healing possible is the same force that makes psychic phenomena in general possible. It may be utilized to make communications between the so-called dead and the living available to those seeking them, or it it may be used in one of several ways as the driving power behind physical phenomena, clairvoyance, psychometry, and the entire range of ESP phenomena. The choice is the user's.[7]

Nandor Fodor states that where psychic healing is concerned, "more frequently the diagnosis and cure take place through spirit influence, advice or direct action."[8]

Healers universally claim they are channels for higher powers. They do not know how their healing works, where it really comes from, what it is, or how to control it. The application form for the American Spiritual Healing Association states: "All healer members must willingly accept the following philosophic statement and standard of conduct: I believe that the source of all healings is a higher or supernatural power which one may call God and that I am a channel or instrument through which healing may manifest."[9]

There is a similar awareness in the National Federation of Spiritual Healers in Great Britain: "Each healer realizes that he himself is not doing the healing but rather is being used as a channel through which the healing is to manifest from a higher source of intelligence."[10]

Whether a healer admits to the supernatural aspect of his healing or not, it is evident he is tapping into the same source. In fact, healers are more like *devices* than channels. A channel is something simply used, whereas a device is intelligently manipulated. The power working through the healers is literally in control of their lives, and they are not really free agents, much as they may believe they are. Even if they want to, they are unable to stop using the power, as we saw with Edgar Cayce. When they attempt to stop, circumstances force them back, or they suffer in various ways until they return to their work. So Gary K. North states of Cayce:

> His biographers seldom refer to the fact that throughout the remainder of his life—forty-five years—Cayce had recurring voice failures. He was completely dependent upon his trance state and its circulation stimulation to return his waking voice to normal. No one could give a physiological reason for the loss of his voice. Those familiar with demon possession would immediately recognize the cause: occult bondage. Cayce could not abandon the physical 'readings' once they had begun. He was trapped.[11]

Psychic healers suffer spiritually and are able to turn to Christ only with the greatest difficulty—if at all. They also may suffer physically during the healing process, temporarily assuming the bodily conditions of the patient and acutely experiencing the ailments.[12]

THE HEALERS — BACKGROUNDS AND METHODS

We turn now to a study of five healers, selected because of their prominence and impact, the documentation of their supernatural abilities, and their diversity of methods and beliefs. Although we believe all psychic healing has but one source, we wish to show the differing viewpoints among the healers themselves as to the sources of their power. The healers we have chosen to examine are Rolling Thunder, Olga Worrall, "Mr. A.," Harry Edwards, and Lawrence LeShan.

ROLLING THUNDER

Rolling Thunder is a spiritual leader and acknowledged spokesman for the Shoshone and Cherokee tribes. Native American, or Indian, healing is often though not entirely shamanistic; common methods involve healing crystals, the help of departed spirits, and so on. Krippner and Villoldo describe the shamanist tradition of Rolling Thunder in their book *The Realms of Healing*:

> Rolling Thunder, however, appears to fall most clearly into the shamanistic tradition with its emphasis upon altered conscious states in which *out-of-body* experiences occur and one travels to another world. These reports are commonly heard by those who study with Rolling Thunder.
>
> Furthermore, the Shoshone medicine man reportedly has communicated with various types of

"spirits" and has demonstrated purported paranormal powers as well. Rolling Thunder's reputed occasional use of "psychic surgery" resembles Eliade's notation that the North American shaman will sometimes appear to extract objects from a sick person's body by suction.[13]

Rolling Thunder has lectured on numerous occasions before legitimate professional groups. He was the principle speaker at the Menninger Foundation's Third Annual Conference at Council Grove, involving participants from five nations. Like other psychics, he claims to receive his power from "the Great Spirit" (God) and that he is merely an instrument, having no special power of his own. He states, "Many times I don't know what medicine I'm going to use until the 'doctoring' is going on; I sometimes can't remember what I've used. That's because it's not me doing the 'doctoring.' It's the Great Spirit working through me."[14]

Rolling Thunder's healing methods involve a combination of spiritism, magic, and shamanism. For example, in healing a patient of a painful, discolored, and infected leg injury, he first inhaled four times, each time praying aloud to the Four Winds (or points on the compass), and then began a loud chanting. He suddenly plunged his head to the wound and began sucking on it. With mouth tightly closed, he moved to a basin and vomited. That process was repeated several times. Then, after rubbing his hands together, he placed them on the wound. He removed an eagle feather from his hat and made long sweeping motions over the patient's body (like the mesmerist hand passes or "energy channeling" of applied kinesiologists), several times shaking off the feather at a piece of raw meat. (The Eagle is his totem bird, having a corresponding spirit guide.)[15]

It is important to recognize that if you or I were to treat that patient and duplicate exactly the methods of Rolling Thunder, the patient would not be healed. It is not the means or procedure used that heals the person; it is the fact that the healer is an occultist. As with the removal of "blood and guts" in psychic surgery and the prescribing of massive (and often unsafe) doses of medicine in psychic diagnosis, that is all "show" for the patient's psychological, not physical, benefit. Rolling Thunder did not suck the poison from the patient's leg—that action and the vomiting were merely to make the patient think so. Likewise shaking off the poison into the meat was pure mumbo-jumbo. The actual healing was done by spirit agency, as Rolling Thunder admits.

In contrast, anyone who would follow the exact procedures of a medical surgeon in an operation or in diagnosis *would* end up with the same results. The distinction between occult and scientific methods is crucial.

OLGA WORRALL

Medium Olga Worrall is one of the psychic healers most studied by parapsychologists. She is very popular as a lecturer on holistic health as well. Her late husband, Ambrose, was also a healer, and they worked as a team. Like most mediums she has had psychic experiences from childhood. Both she and Ambrose had regular visits from "the dead" as part of their upbringing. With Olga they started at age three.[16]

In keeping with the current trend of redefining the occult, Olga states that she does not do *psychic* healing, she does *spiritual* healing. Olga has healed on hundreds of occasions and claims her complete healings run at 50 percent. Whether that includes the horses, cats, birds, and dogs she heals as well is unknown. (Incidentally, the healing of animals by psychic healers rules out suggestion as the explanation of the cure, although it is also true that religious suggestion may be the cause for a great deal of purported modern "healings.") The Worralls believe they are instruments of the Holy Spirit: "Above all, we are grateful for the opportunity to watch the power of the Holy Spirit at work in the everyday world of so many men, women and children."[17] As with the rest of their psychic family around the Western world, whenever they quote the Bible to support either their "gift" or occult world view, it is invariably out of context or obviously misapplied.[18]

Unfortunately, the Worralls began their healing ministry with children. Occult bondage comes easily then, since children are so trusting. The resultant spiritual perversion those children will experience later on is matched only by the severe ignorance of those who think psychic healing can in any sense be ultimately beneficial to children, or adults for that matter. Eventually the Worralls worked out of the New Life Clinic at the Baltimore, Maryland, Washington Methodist Church, where Olga is still healing people who come from far and wide, seeking relief from their physical problems. In addition, every night she engages in "distant healing" (nonpsychometric). That activity involves thousands of people who have written to her for help. Recipients report feeling a tingling sensation when being healed. That "pins and needles" feeling is exceptionally common among occultists of all types and those they heal or otherwise contact, and is perhaps evidence of demonic energizing. Olga, like so many others, says the "power" is not hers: ". . . the spiritual power comes from God. I put my hands on someone and pray, but it is God who does the work . . . why should it tire me? The power comes from spiritual sources, not from me."[19]

In their book *The Gift of Healing*, the Worralls describe the process of meditation by which the healing power is developed. Its pantheistic flavor is evident:

> Continuing his contemplation by waiting alert for further knowledge, he becomes more and more aware of his affinity with the Supreme Being, until at last he reaches the realization that all are one, and the full significance of the words, 'The Father dwelleth in me and I in Him,' dawns upon his awakened spiritual consciousness, and he says, yes, indeed.[20] [At the 1978 holistic health conference in San Diego, she stated John 10:30 was true for everyone and that "God is in all things."—Authors]

After her husband died, Olga started getting messages from him via "the spirit plane." In reality, that is a quite common phenomenon among occultists and is a key tactic in spiritual deception. After a close friend or relative dies, demons impersonating him often "come back" to "help and guide the loved ones left on earth" to "prove survival" and communicate about "the next life, and how wrong all those concepts of heaven and hell were" or, to "help progress on the earthly plane." In every case the impact is to deny the biblical world view and promote a false sense of spiritual security (universalism). The late "Ambrose" claims that he now works through Olga in healing and that "he is being instructed on the spiritual plane in ways to improve the forces used in psychic healing."[21]

Worrall claims she does not use mediumistic powers, but the statement is obviously false. Anyone who contacts or acknowleges the help of the dead is a medium. There are many forms and varieties of mediumship; Olga is not a trance medium, but she contacts the dead routinely. The Worralls' spirit contacts have been in the hundreds and she often sees "the dead" clairvoyantly.[22] "In a normal state," she says, "I am able to hear and see discarnate spirits, and as I hear what the spirit says, I repeat it [for healing]."[23]

The April 1972 issue of *Psychic* magazine contains the last in-depth interview with Ambrose Worrall before his death. In the interview he referred to an unknown power's taking control of his body, and of healing people while under its influence. Olga has similar experiences and refers to "an overwhelming force taking hold of me, drawing on me."[24] Neither of them can control the "power"—they "have no control over the flow of healing current: [we] cannot turn it on."[25] They simply depend on its "being there" when needed, and it usually is. Olga admitted, "I might add that several dedicated doctors in the spirit world work with us. They apparently know how to use the laws governing spiritual healing."[26] Psychic Harold Sherman, who wrote *Your Power to Heal*, a book largely about the Worralls, stated: "The Worralls have given me access to the literally hundreds of reports, testimonials and records of their contact with spirit entities."[27] Mr. Sherman urges that all of us develop the same power the Worralls have, and his naiveté here is surpassed only by his benign irresponsibility in helping to enslave many well-intentioned people to occultism.

Olga Worrall, like many others, may claim she is not a medium and that her powers are godly, but the facts suggest otherwise.

MR. A.

Mr. A. was born in 1895 and from childhood received psychic communications from what he termed the "Powers," personal intelligences who transmit "God's" power and information to him. The palm of his right hand bears the same star markings Jeanne Dixon has.

(For whatever reason, some persons are "marked" in the womb as a result of occult involvement on the parents' part, e.g., Swami Rama was born with a hole in his ear [as predicted]; at least one Hare Krishna baby was born with the red *telak* marks on its face; birthmarks of a recently deceased person may show up on a newborn baby [identical in location and size] as "proof" of reincarnation.)

When medium Ruth Montgomery first wrote of him in *A Search for the Truth*, she received over 10,000 letters from people wanting more information about his healing abilities, philosophy, and source of power.[28]

Like many psychics, when he was five years old, he would go to the woods where he received "psychic instruction." "All the while I was alone, Life and the History of Life were being explained to me in detail, through inner listening. That was my education. What I was receiving was not taught in any schools."[29] His entire life was guided by "the Powers"—they instructed him, healed through him, and made many of his decisions for him. To a significant extent, they controlled many of the events in his life, a factor characteristic of nearly every occultist. Occultists are protected, used, guided to certain people for certain purposes (e.g., to increase their influence), and in general are puppets, though they rarely suspect it.

Dena Smith, M.D., in the foreword to Ruth Montgomery's book on Mr. A., *Born to Heal*, states, "During the past decade I have worked closely with Mr. A, keeping detailed records of many of his cases and subjecting them to intensive scrutiny. I have observed at first-hand his work with thousands of persons suffering from a wide variety of ailments which run the gamut of medical literature, and I have yet to find an instance when the patient was not substantially benefited or healed."[30] Ruth Montgomery is even more bold in assessing his powers. She states that reliable "witnesses, including doctors and nurses, have seen this man stop heart attacks, heal crippled arthritics, dissipate large tumors, arrest glaucoma, and rebuild a disintegrated jawbone, simply by placing his hand on what he terms the *magnetic field*—that is, the lower abdomen or pelvic area."[31] According to Mr. A., that area is a psychic switchboard for the operations of the body:

> In here is an intricate system, grouping together the main trunk nerves and their branches and relay systems which extend throughout the body. The lungs draw in the energy, but the magnetic field must draw the energy from the lungs in order to radiate it through the body. Everything is centered in the belly.[32]

According to Mr. A., physical problems are electromagnetic in origin. Strokes, arthritis, and so on, have their origin "in the magnetic field"—the distributor of energy to the body's organs. All healing is achieved by the energy generated through Mr. A. from "the Powers."[33] He also claims that he can tune into the "universal Ring of Wisdom"—a band of available energy containing all knowledge since time began—in other words, the occult source long known as the Akashic records. (Whatever its ultimate reality, it is a convenient guise for covert demonic activity, and has been so used in hundreds of cases. Levi's *The Aquarian Gospel of Jesus the Christ* is a more well-known example.)

Mr. A. has no medical training and "does not pretend that his knowledge of ailments is within his own conscious mind. When he examines a patient, he tunes to the higher frequency controlled by 'the Powers' and receives guidance directly from them."[34]

Recently, after decades of healing, he decided to "just plain loaf" during his seventieth year. But the spirits had other ideas, and they always get their way. "The Powers ordered me to teach others this age-old method of healing."[35] Mr. A.'s *Life Energies Research Foundation* is now in full operation.

HARRY EDWARDS

Harry Edwards, Britain's most famous healer, received an average of 10,000-12,000 letters *per week*, and upon his death in 1976 was still receiving 10,000 letters per year for absent healing alone.[36] His influence has been as vast as it has been tragic. According to George Meek, "The existence in England of the National Federation of Spiritual Healers with its thousands of healers, and the fact that governing authorities of 1,500 hospitals also permit entry of Federation members to visit patients, are both a tribute to the many decades of pioneering work in the field of healing by Harry Edwards."[37] But Kurt Koch calls him "one of the most dangerous healers of the Western world."[38]

Harry Edwards became involved in healing through attending seances. He eventually received spirit guides and did all of his healing, as he admitted, by their power. He had no power apart from them. In an address before the Anglican church's Commission on Divine Healing, he said: "By a spiritual or divine healing, I mean a healing that is brought about by a non-human agency. I define a healer as a person who is used as an instrument for healing by a non-human agency and that he (of himself) possesses no personal ability to heal."[39]

His books include *A Guide to Spirit Healing*, *Thirty Years a Spiritual Healer*, *Agenda to the Understanding and Practice of Spiritual Healing*, and others, most published by the Spiritualist Press in England.

Dr. Koch comments on the influence of such a man, and the apathy that allowed such copious occultism to go unchecked:

> In spite of the Bible designating spiritism as the cult of the devil, and in spite of it condemning those who take part in spiritistic practices, here is a man who, after having taken part in hundreds of spiritistic meetings, still claims to be a channel of divine power. It seems unimaginable that genuine Christians should ever resort to such a person for help, and yet while counselling people in England I came across the case of a British missionary actually sending her own mother to Harry Edwards in order to obtain healing. What terrible shortsightedness and irresponsibility.
>
> But quite obviously healings do take place. The question is, what is the force behind the healings? We have many passages in the Bible recording the ability of sorcerers to work miracles. We need only think of the Egyptian magicians who opposed Moses in Exodus 7, or of the demonic signs and wonders mentioned in Matthew 24:24, Mark 13:22, 2 Thessalonians 2:9 and Revelation 13:13 and 16:14. Every person healed through the influence of mediumistic forces though, suffers a deathlike blow to his faith. He falls victim to a kind of spiritistic ban. And this will be particularly tragic in the case of the many hundreds of ministers and clergymen who have turned to Harry Edwards for this extremely doubtful type of help.
>
> Edwards has rendered the British people a dreadful service. Thousands upon thousands of people have been burdened through the work of this prophet of spiritistic spirits. And yet the Christians in England remain silent. [40]

LAWRENCE LESHAN

Psychologist Lawrence LeShan is a key figure in psychic healing. Since he has a reputable academic background, many people listen to his ideas and research who otherwise would never consider it. His popular first book, *The Medium, the Mystic and the Physicist,* is one of the serious works tying together "science" and the occult. Like Dr. Tiller, he is a prototype of the "New Consciousness" man— intellectual, occultic, spiritually evolved, forward-looking, pantheist advocate of "the one," hopeful of the "new age." As a parapsychologist, he has spent literally hundreds of hours conversing with the control spirits of trance mediums, and his development of psychic healing methods was in part dependent on his study of mediums and how they heal.[41]

As a self-taught healer, Dr. LeShan has developed a program to train other psychic healers. He has divided all occult healers into two categories, Type I and Type II. His concern is primarily with the former. These have several common characteristics, for example, using altered states of consciousness and what he calls the prayer method, in which the healer through "love" psychically merges with the patient.[42] Dr. LeShan states: "At that moment the healer is perceiving in the deepest sense that the universe is constituted on other lines, that we're all one. The patient . . . is merged with the healer as part of it. . . . All is one. Nothing is alone."[43]

LeShan also says, "The healer does not 'do' or 'give' something to the healee; instead he helps him come home to the All, to the One, to the way of 'unity' with the Universe, and in this 'meeting' the healee becomes more complete and this in itself is healing."[44]

He notes that during the healing he is aware that the "All" is the "One" is "God," and that at those moments that unity becomes clear.[45] Such pantheistic philosophies are found among all occultists, as well as in some drug and insane states.[46] Whether they result from a psychic misperception of God's omnipresence or spiritual warfare, they are seriously deceptive as to the true nature of reality. Once the distinction between Creator/creature is abandoned, biblical salvation is abandoned, because if everything is one, nothing (man and God for instance) is separated.

However, LeShan, in a revealing statement, tells us how closely his methods tie in with those of mediums. A member of the audience queried:

Q. "How can you say your theory applies to a Spiritualist healer like Harry Edwards?"

A. "He does the same merging of self with patient. It's the same procedure with a different explanation system."[47]

LeShan did not become a healer overnight. As is often the case, study and discipline were essential, and various occult writings and personal meditation were of great help:

> I had therefore to teach myself to go into an altered state of consciousness of a particular type. For at least a moment, I had to *know* that. . . . All is One, and to do this somehow 'centered' about the uniting of another person and myself in the clairvoyant reality.[48]

Today, he teaches others what he has learned and so far has taught scores, if not hundreds, of people to become psychic healers. He notes that it has become easier to teach others how to enter altered states of consciousness and that the techniques have been perfected enough so that virtually anyone could enter an altered state. (Again, however, not everyone was or is able to become a psychic healer; the implication is that it is not really a latent, natural capacity everyone can develop.) LeShan's basic program involves three types of psychic exercises;

mind-training, exercises to help abandon the concept of time and space, and specific regimens leading step by step to the particular state of consciousness associated with psychic healing.

The shattering of time-space concepts has always
been a central aspect for advancement in the occult.
When men function in ordinary reality, they cannot
enter the world of the occult; hence from time im-
memorial the cultivation of non-ordinary states of
reality has been essential for occult purposes.
Whether the method used is drugs (Castanada),
meditation (TM), or LeShan's, the essential part is to
escape the normal environment and open oneself to
another world.

The consequences are always grave. In the case
of LeShan the results have been to make his world
view pantheist and amoral. The latter is clearly indicated when he says:

> I do not believe that the universe is concerned with
> our standards of good and evil. Electricity is neutral;
> it can be used to help or to kill. So, too, it seems to
> me, are the rest of the energies of the universe.
>
> There is certainly a widespread belief among
> many religious people that 'God is good.' I do not
> understand this statement. It seems at best a tre-
> mendous reduction, a bringing down to our value
> system of something far beyond it.

And yet he says:

> Nevertheless, I do not believe it is possible to use
> these energies to harm.[49]

Such a belief is itself dangerous—as those "energies" have been used to maim or murder tens of
thousands, if not millions of people worldwide. They
are no more ethically neutral than the lord of darkness himself. Demonic energy cannot be removed
from the demon using it, regardless of its actual na-

ture. Whatever energy operates in a seance, the *purpose* is always to bring bondage and deception. And that is the crux of the issue of the use of energy: purpose. Once you have purposed to use a gun to kill, or the atom for a bomb, the energy is no longer ethically neutral. The moment a knife is picked up by a murderer, it undergoes a teleological change. Objects or things are only neutral when they are not being used, or when no purpose is intended for them. Man's very existence—particularly fallen man's—leaves very little ethically neutral. How much more so in the demonic realm!

In the area of psychic healing and other uses of demonic energy, since the purpose is *always* occult bondage, the energy has never been ethically neutral, practically speaking. If man has been unable to keep the atom neutral—indeed he seems ready to blow himself up[50]—how can he possibly do the same with *intelligent* energies that act *strategically* against him, especially when we consider that man's knowledge of the atom is encyclopedic compared to his understanding of psychic energies? It has been said that psychic power is even more dangerous than atomic power. The statement is accurate and cause for concern. The consequences in the lives of all those thousands of people healed mediumistically by LeShan and his occult students are biblically of the severest nature—consequences that extend beyond time itself, "because God will bring every act to judgment, everything which is hidden, whether it is good or evil. . . . According to their deeds, so He will repay" (Ecclesiastes 12:14; Isaiah 59:18).

Aligning oneself with forces opposed to the infinite, personal God of the universe is no small matter. The fact that LeShan found that most people could be trained to become effective psychic healers[51] itself points to why the Bible warns against occult involvement. Anyone can *choose* to align himself with forces odious to God, and if he works hard enough he will probably get results. The fact that most are unaware of the personal and ultimate nature of those forces does not discount the forces' eagerness to be used. And that use, apart from repentance and turning to Christ, always results in the user's ultimate destruction.

HEALERS — CHANNELS FOR SUPERNATURAL POWERS

Modern healers are said to exercise the power of various types of *magnetic healing* or *laying on of hands* (the psychic version, as distinguished from the biblically sanctioned practice). Those methods are simply another style of psychic healing. For example, the Theosophical Research Center's publication *The Mysteries of Healing* points out:

> [All these methods] involve the transference of vital and possibly spiritual energies by and through the practitioner to the patient by means of the hands, the breath, or his mere presence. . . . The healer may use the forces of his own personality, adding to them perhaps by auto-suggestion and thereby analyzing the latent but readily available vitality of the atmosphere. One type of healer draws upon the vitality of persons who may be near, thus merely acting as a means of conveying the vitality of a group to his patient. Another type will have contact with healing angels or devas [spirits, gods] who readily co-operate in such work, but of whom the healer may be entirely unaware. Any strong magnetic healer in all probability has attendants in the unseen worlds, who are more likely to be devic than human.[52]

The above descriptions of drawing energy from the air, group vampirism, and so on, are close enough to the descriptions given by occultists to cause doubt upon the supposed benevolence of their sources. The book also defines the controllers of those energies:

> From the viewpoint of this book, angels or devas are recognized as agents for the concentration and distribution of psycho-spiritual energies. They are considered to be intelligent beings of a non-human order of nature that runs parallel to the human kingdom. They work unseen in the subtle, and hence invisible worlds . . . the human mind can give clear and useful direction to these healing forces supplied by angelic workers. Such co-operation is intended, and healing work gives a great opportunity for its expression.[53]

The conclusions of the book are that spirits are the ones governing the use of that energy, and that in all cases the energy is drawn either from the surrounding environment, people close by, the healer himself, or the spirit world. And that is the very essence of occultism.

The above descriptions are a clear indication of the mediumistic nature of psychic healing—some created thing must have energy taken from it to produce the healing. Like men, demons cannot create energy; they can only utilize and change pre-existing forms. In contrast, biblical healing utilizes God's power; healing energy does not need to be drawn from any other source. His power is inexhaustible and works through the one doing the healing, never needing to utilize surrounding energy. The healings of Christ and the apostles, therefore, were instantaneous and complete, rather than gradual and partial, as are most occult healings. That contrast between godly versus occult healings is important to recognize. It is apparent often enough to suggest that we are dealing with two entirely different worlds of healing.

Again, the presence of spirits is virtually certain in all cases of occult healing, though they are often not sensed or recognized, as the above quoted publication states:

> The term *vital magnetic healing* is employed to describe the conscious use of vital energy, drawn from almost any source, which is conveyed to the patient largely through the healer's hands. . . . All that has been said about the various sources from which vital energy can be drawn for the laying on of hands applies to this method, as does also the description of the different types of healers. It is frequently employed by "spirit healers," working "under control," and is then sometimes described as "power" from the loftiest levels of existence.[54]

The book also points out that under the categories of *mental* and *absent* healing, "a dedicated worker can call upon the help from agencies in the unseen worlds."[55] That is true for all other methods of occult healings as well, of course.

HEALING PLACES—THE SHRINES

For ages certain locations or temples have been said to be centers of healing. Such places were much more numerous in the ancient world, and nearly always associated with the various gods that reportedly inhabited them. Merrill F. Unger states:

> The world in which the early Christians lived was full of demons and demon-energized healers and magic workers (Acts 8:9-11; 13:7-10). In the temple of Serapis at Alexandria Egypt, multitudes of pagans were remarkably healed. Pilgrimages to Epidaurus

in Greece became world famous, and a night's sleep in the sacred temple cured thousands.[56]

Walter Jayne, M.D., in his *Healing Gods of Ancient Civilizations* reports on many of the gods of Egypt, Babylonia, Assyria, India, Greece, and Rome, and the cures attributed to them at their shrines. Sufferers thronged to the temples of Imhotep of Egypt (2700 B.C.). Shrines of Aesculapius, the Greek god of healing, were associated with a serpent cult, and thus the god was transported from shrine to shrine in the form of snakes. He would heal many who slept in his temples—provided they were not bitten first, we presume. Oftentimes at the various temples the spirits would prescribe cures for the sick in their dreams, or through oracles (possessed people who would speak for the god). Even Apollo took second place to Aesculapius, and the cult proved a definite obstacle to early Christianity.

The two modern healing locations we wish to briefly mention are the shrines of Fatima (Portugal) and Lourdes (France), although there are many others. The stories behind their origins are too detailed to mention here and several books have already been written on the subject. We can say, however, that both fit the pattern of demonic methodology that can be observed in hundreds of cases of the origin of occult movements. Both originated by visions of one claiming to be Mary, the Mother of God, and the messages she gave were distinctly opposed to the Bible, further validating the demonic nature of those shrines and their healings. At both Fatima and Lourdes, "Mary" encouraged belief in nonbiblical doctrines—the sinlessness and worship of Mary, her intercession between God and man, the use of rosaries, and so on.[57]

Although some Christians believe God does heal at those shrines,[58] we find it difficult to suppose that the Holy Spirit (whose central purpose is to glorify Christ and convict men of their need to trust solely in Him) would authenticate theological error by supernatural manifestations.

A good discussion of the miracles at Lourdes, Fatima, and elsewhere can be found in Benjamin Warfield's *Counterfeit Miracles*.[59] He quotes Herbert Thurston as stating "undoubtedly the greatest stimulus to Marian devotion in recent times has been afforded by the apparition of the Blessed Virgin in 1858 at Lourdes."[60] Pilgrims there have numbered in the tens of millions. Warfield states:

> Even though we should stand dumb before the wonders of Lourdes, and should be utterly incapable of suggesting a natural causation for them, we know right well that they are not of God. The whole complex of circumstances of which they are a part; their origin in occurrences, the best that can be said of which is that they are silly; their intimate connection with a cult derogatory to the rights of God who alone is to be called upon in our distresses, stamp them, prior to all examination of the mode of their occurrence, as not from God. We are far more sure that they are not from God than we ever can be sure, after whatever scrutiny, of precisely how they are wrought. . . .
>
> "The whole place," says Benson, "is alive with Mary." That is the very reason why we are sure the marvels which occur there are not the direct acts of God, but are of the same order as the similar ones which have occurred at many similar shrines, of many names, in many lands, serving many gods."[61]

The Mysteries of Healing publication also notes the presence of spirits at such shrines and adds that "in some very primitive communities, such [healing] localities are used for magical purposes and forms of worship along animistic lines; these may even include blood sacrifice. The healing forces so invoked at times involve the death of a selected victim, animal or human, or possibly the devitalizing of a child or relative."[62]

CONCLUSION

In conclusion, psychic healing is not a part of the natural or latent capacities of man. It is a distinctly supernatural, spiritistic power and carries grave consequences both for those who practice it and for those healed by it. Those who practice it may have no indication that spirit entities are the real source of their power, but that does not reduce their own responsibility for the spiritual and psychological destruction of those they heal. There is always a high price to pay when contacting forces alien to God.

NOTES

1. Merrill F. Unger, *Demons in the World Today*, p. 138; Walter Jayne, *The Healing Gods of Ancient Civilizations.*
2. Kurt Koch, *The Devil's Alphabet*, p. 104; J. Rindge, "Perspective—An Overview of Paranormal Healing," in George W. Meek, ed., *Healers and the Healing Process*, p. 15.
3. C. Norman Shealy, "Postscript," in Meek, p. 265.
4. Rindge, in Meek, p. 17.
5. Hans Naegeli-Osjord, "Psychiatric and Psychological Considerations," in Meek, p. 80.
6. Hans Holzer, *Beyond Medicine*, pp. 43-84.
7. Ibid., p. 161.
8. Nandor Fodor, "Psychic Healing," in *Encyclopaedia of Psychic Science*, p. 167.
9. Membership brochure, American Spiritual Healing Association, pp. 5-6.

10. Gilbert Anderson, "Paranormal Healing in Great Britain," in Meek, p. 51.
11. Gary K. North, *None Dare Call It Witchcraft*, p. 117.
12. Fodor, p. 167.
13. Stanley Krippner and Alberto Villoldo, *The Realms of Healing*, pp. 108-9.
14. Ibid., pp. 56-57.
15. Doug Boyd, *Rolling Thunder*, chapter 2; Krippner and Villoldo, pp. 55-70.
16. Ambrose A. Worrall and Olga N. Worrall, *The Gift of Healing*, pp. 13-15.
17. Ibid., p. 206.
18. See for example Olga Worrall in Academy of Parapsychology and Medicine, *The Dimensions of Healing: A Symposium*, p. 23.
19. Krippner and Villoldo, p. 92.
20. Worrall and Worrall, pp. 186-87.
21. Krippner and Villoldo, p. 96.
22. Harold Sherman, *Your Power to Heal;* Worrall and Worrall, pp. 125, 141.
23. Sherman, p. 69.
24. Worrall and Worrall, p. 124.
25. Sherman, p. 186.
26. Ibid., pp. 186-87, 192.
27. Ibid., p. 143.
28. Ruth Montgomery, *Born to Heal*, p. 36.
29. Ibid., p. 41.
30. Ibid., p. 11.
31. Ruth Montgomery, *A Search for the Truth*, p. 175.
32. Ibid.
33. Montgomery, *Born to Heal*, pp. 16-17.
34. Montgomery, *A Search for the Truth*, pp. 185-86.
35. Ibid., p. 190.
36. George W. Meek, "The Healers," in Meek, p. 31; Sally Hammond, *We Are All Healers*, p. 127; Kurt

Koch, *Occult Bondage and Deliverance.*

37. Meek, p. 31.
38. Koch, *Occult Bondage*, p. 44.
39. Hammond, p. 122.
40. Koch, *Occult Bondage*, pp. 46-47. Copyright 1970 by Kregel Publications. Used by permission.
41. Lawrence LeShan, *The Medium, the Mystic, and the Physicist*, pp. 103-4.
42. Ibid., p. 106.
43. Hammond, p. 253.
44. LeShan, p. 110.
45. Ibid., p. 148.
46. John Weldon and Zola Levitt, *The Transcendental Explosion*, chapters 4-6.
47. Hammond, p. 256.
48. LeShan, p. 113.
49. Ibid., pp. 160-61.
50. See Clifford Wilson and John Weldon, *1980s: Decade of Shock.*
51. LeShan, p. 130.
52. Theosophical Research Centre, *The Mystery of Healing*, p. 52.
53. Ibid., pp. 77-78.
54. Ibid., pp. 54-55.
55. Ibid., p. 57.
56. Unger, p. 138.
57. For a comparison of biblical versus Catholic beliefs see Loraine Boettner, *Roman Catholicism.*
58. Unger, pp. 139-40.
59. Benjamin B. Warfield, *Counterfeit Miracles*, pp. 99-124.
60. Ibid., p. 103.
61. Ibid., pp. 122-23.
62. Theosophical Research Centre, *The Mystery of Healing*, p. 72.

6

Psychic Surgery

When we come into the realm of psychic surgery, we may seem to be stepping over into fairy tales. Probably the majority of those who hear reports on psychic surgery simply smile indulgently. The whole area is widely considered to be one of fraud—the work of clever magicians who extract high profits from some truly amazing illusions.

However, we shall adhere to the philosophy we have been establishing—simply that mediumistic abilities are at work here, and even more powerful ones than those involved in psychic healing or diagnosis. Undoubtedly some trickery is involved, and we shall document that, but it is impossible to ignore the multitude of astonishing medical feats established before witnesses of unquestionable repute. Something decidedly beyond common medical practice is at work here.

We shall quote profusely in this chapter from other sources. Due to the controversy and downright strangeness of the subject, a variety of investigators have been consulted and a wide selection of their observations are reproduced.

On the subject of mediumistic abilities in general,

and psychic surgery in particular, we must begin by saying that the latter requires an abundance of the former. Apparently a better medium is needed to perform surgery than to heal nonsurgically or to diagnose an illness. Few mediums have the power required to perform this incredible surgery, and it should be noted that no phenomenon of psychic surgery has ever been produced apart from the presence of a medium.

FORMS OF "SURGERY"

As with psychic diagnosis and healing, there are also several forms of psychic surgery. In one type, the surgeon is said to operate on the "etheric" body and does not touch the physical body. He works with invisible surgical instruments, aided by "spirit doctors" on "the other side." In a second form, the surgeon *psychically* opens the body (without a knife) and removes "tumors," "diseased tissue," and so on. Others use various crude instruments (as common pocketknives) to make the incisions and perform the surgery. Often there is a combination of two or more methods.

PSYCHIC SURGERY SPECIALISTS

There are also "specialists," both of method and type of operation. For example, the celebrated Arigo's specialty was eye operations. In all cases the surgeon is in a mediumistic trance, and the one actually performing the operation is the spirit guide. That is openly acknowledged by all psychic surgeons, and they admit they can do nothing apart from their other-worldly help. Edivaldo is representative:"I don't invoke anything. The spirits just come.

I sit down and withdraw my own spirit and Dr. Cala-
zans takes over. There isn't room for two spirits in one
body, you see."[1]

FRAUD

In any discussion of psychic surgery the question
of fraud always arises. Fakery clearly exists in all
forms of psychic healing—including psychic
surgery. Charges of fraud are levied more often
against psychic surgery because it is much harder
to believe in; however, it is clearly true that supernatural manifestations do occur in legitimate psychic surgery. Several of the most popular books have
documented both the fraud and the reality: Tom
Valentine's *Psychic Surgery*, John Fuller's *Arigo: The
Surgeon of the Rusty Knife*, Harold Sherman's
"Wonder" Healer of the Philippines, Pedro McGreg-
gor's *Jesus of the Spirits*, Guy Playfair's *The Unknown Power*, and others. According to testimonials,
psychic surgery has cured blindness, most types of
cancer, eye tumors (sometimes the eye is entirely
removed from its socket), and many other critical
ailments.[2]

OPERATING CONDITIONS

In many ways, psychic surgery is the opposite of
medical surgery. Operations are performed in unsanitary and even filthy environments; there is an
utter lack of medical training on the part of the surgeons; no anesthesia is used; dirty or rusty knives
are common surgical instruments; the surgeon pays
little attention to his work—he may literally be looking away while his hand is twisting a knife in a
patient's eye. In spite of all those bizarre conditions,

the patient has no pain, is often healed, and the flesh is opened and closed with no hemorrhage— sometimes even without a scar!

THE SURGEONS

The majority of psychic surgeons come from the spiritist centers of Brazil and the Philippines. The best known include Arigo, who attended 300 to 400 people a day—more than 2,000,000 before his fatal accident; Tony Agpaoa, who attends 100 per day; Lourival de Freitas, who performed his first surgery at age five[3] and who drinks an entire bottle of Scotch whiskey before operating; Maria, who always operates with her eyes closed; Antonio Sales, Zeca, Josephina Sison, Marcelo Jainer, Felisa Macanas, Jose Mercado, Romy and Joe Bugarin, Edivaldo, Terte, Blance, and Ading.

Pyschic surgery has even come to America, though in a milder form. The Reverend Harold G. Plume of California uses the same operating techniques as the Philippine surgeons, but in less bloody fashion. He thrusts his hands into the body (usually only the fingers), but he operates *through* the clothing. Gary K. North states:

> Like Tony Agpaoa, who had visions as a youth, Plume had visions. But he had them at age three, which may be a record of some kind. People would appear to him in his room. He saw the disembodied spirits of the departed. He is now controlled by a Chinese physician who lived 2,500 years ago. His name is Hoo-Fang. Honest. And he does something even Dr. Fritz and Agpaoa's "protector" never tried: he operates right through clothing. Complete modesty prevails in his church; he is British, not some simple barbarian. Things are done properly. Furthermore, he inserts only his fingers whenever pos-

sible, not his hands, plus a piece of Kleenex. There is no muss, no fuss, and no blood. Ladies in knit dresses bought in California shops do not appreciate bloody performances. (Agpaoa is unique in this respect; he loves a bloody show.)[4]

Psychic surgery embraces a wide variety of different phenomena. The best way to gain an overall view is to quote descriptions of the surgeons' work.

JOSEFINA SISON

I came to this woman [Sison] in great pain and agony. I walked in to her, told her what it was, laid face down on the wooden table, and within thirty seconds she removed a cyst which looked like a pigeon's egg. When I stood up, the pain was all gone and there was no scar. That was three days ago and I have not had pain since. . . . When Josefina was asked how she knows what is wrong with the patients, she said, "There are three stages of knowing. In most cases I can tell with my 'third eye' [clairvoyantly]. In more difficult cases, I feel that my hands are guided to the area needing attention and I hear a voice in my ear. In extremely difficult cases, I do both these and in addition I sit down and do some automatic writing. As soon as the pencil moves along the paper, I know what the pencil is writing and it may be a great surprise to me."[5]

Stanley Krippner, a well-known psychologist and parapsychologist, decided to have "surgery" performed on himself by Josephina Sison:

I unbuttoned my shirt, . . . lying down on the wooden table with my head on a Bible. Sison bowed her head in prayer and folded her hands. As she opened her hands, I could see that the fingers were wide apart. As the hands came down on my abdominal area, small red drops of fluid began to appear. Soon, streams of red fluid trickled down my sides.

The fluid appeared to come from the part of my skin which came into direct contact with Sison's hands. There were no clotlike objects and she later took this to mean that the ailment was not serious.

After wiping her hands and my abdomen with cotton, Sison tore a fresh piece of cotton from a roll and dipped it in coconut oil. Earlier, she had claimed that coconut oil was used by "psychic surgeons" for "healing" because "it helps direct the power of the Holy Spirit." Sison pressed the wad of cotton, which measured about one inch by half an inch, to the right side of my body. Sison moved her hands carefully and they seemed to be empty. Again, the fingers were not pressed together and the palms were open.

As Sison brought her fingers to my side, a piece of cotton appeared to protrude from my skin. She began to pull it up and I could see that it was streaked with red. I moved my body to get a better look. Sison stopped pulling, removing her hand from the cotton. And for that moment, the cotton appeared to be sticking halfway out of my body. Then she finished removing the cotton and I could see traces of red fluid on either side of it—but no coconut oil. She told me that the fluid was "impure blood" and that the coconut oil remained in my body to complete the "healing" process.[6]

Due to its clearly supernatural nature, psychic surgery often leaves observers literally stunned.

ARIGO

John Fuller, in his book concerning Arigo, describes the impact the psychic surgeon's eye operations had on parapsychologist and UFO contactee Andrija Puharich, M.D.:

Suddenly and without ceremony, he roughly took the first man in line—an elderly, well-dressed gentleman in an impeccable gray sharkskin suit—firmly grasped his shoulders, and held him against the wall, directly under the sign THINK OF JESUS. Puharich, standing next to the man, was startled by the action, wondered what to expect next.

Then, without a word, Arigo picked up a four-inch stainless steel paring knife with a cocobolo-wood handle, and literally plunged it into the man's left eye, under the lid and deep into the eye socket.

In spite of his years of medical practice and experience, Puharich was shocked and stunned. He was even more so when Arigo began violently scraping the knife between the ocular globe and the inside of the lid, pressing up into the sinus area with uninhibited force. The man was wide awake, fully conscious, and showed no fear whatsoever. He did not move or flinch. A woman in the background screamed. Another fainted. Then Arigo levered the eye so that it extended from the socket. The patient, still utterly calm, seemed bothered by only one thing: a fly that had landed on his cheek. At the moment his eye was literally tilted out of its socket, he calmly brushed the fly away from his cheek.

As he made these motions, Arigo hardly looked at his subject, and at one point turned away to address an assistant while his hand continued to scrape and plunge without letup. In another moment, he turned away from the patient completely, letting the knife dangle half out of the eye.

Then he turned abruptly to Puharich and asked him to place his finger on the eyelid, so that he could feel the point of the knife under the skin. By this time, Puharich was almost in a state of shock but he did so, clearly feeling the point of the knife through the skin. Quickly, Puharich asked one of the interpreters to ask the patient what he felt. The patient spoke calmly and without excitement, merely stating that although he was well aware of the knife, he felt no pain or discomfort.[7]

The diagnostic power of the surgeons is obviously supernatural. Dr. Puharich comments on the illiterate Arigo:

(Another aspect of Arigo's diagnostic ability has become, for me, a paradigm of certain extrasensory perception phenomena. I uncovered this while observing Arigo perform a series of approximately 1,000 diagnoses, in which a phenomenal number were accurate. I was particularly impressed with his command of precise medical terminology. For example, rather than saying that the patient was suffering from eye trouble, Arigo diagnosed it as retinoblastoma, or retinitis pigmentosa, etc. When Arigo saw my amazement, he said, "This is one of the simpler tasks for me because I simply listen to a voice in my right ear and repeat what is says."). . .

Arigo was able to prescribe every known modern pharmacological agent, and often what he prescribed had no rational connection with the ailment, in the light of conventional medicine. Our medical research team was highly impressed by the range of knowledge which Arigo demonstrated in using this molecular matching procedure, and in particular, with his ability to treat not only the immediate problem, but the root cause of it.[8]

Guy L. Playfair also comments on Arigo's amazing ability:

To Arigo, it was a matter of doing the job in hand as quickly as possible and getting on with the next one, working standing up for hours on end without showing signs of fatigue. He never seemed to pause to think. He would casually prod the patient with one hand while scribbling off a complicated prescription with the other. He could deal with consultations at the rate of one a minute; diagnosis, prescription and all. As to the accuracy of the diagnoses, Dr. Puharich and his team were able to follow up several hundred cases and confirm Arigo's findings as 95% correct. What first strikes everybody who is able to witness psychic surgery is the amazing speed at which some, but not all, surgeons work, and the complete self-confidence they all show in the process. The impression really is of another force guiding their hands, especially when, as so often happens, they are not even looking at what their hands are doing.[9]

Fuller also described a case of advanced stomach cancer that was completely healed:

> Arigo took him into the small, almost-vacant room behind his general working area. He laid him down on the crude wooden door stretched between two sawhorses. Then Arigo began pressing down on his stomach with both hands. Juvenal experienced no pain, just a feeling of heavy pressure and considerable discomfort. Arigo pressed with all his beefy weight, until it seemed as if the stomach wall would be pushed against the spinal column. Suddenly the stomach popped with a clearly audible sound, like the cork of a champagne bottle. There was blood, but there was no hemorrhage. Arigo reached into the upper abdomen with his hands and literally pulled out a large quantity of what Juvenal described as "bloody things." Arigo used no instrument. Juvenal felt apprehensive, but still no pain.
>
> When Arigo removed his hands, the wound closed immediately, with no stitches. Juvenal felt weak and shaken, but was able to get up and walk out of the room.[10]

FELISA MACANAS

Felisa Macanas removed a piece of glass embedded below the muscle fibers of the hand in a "biblical" way:

> After a few moments of attunement [meditation], Felisa's altered breathing indicated she had entered into a very light trance state. . . . She gently moved her fingers over the area for perhaps half a minute. Then she asked her husband to hold the open Bible, face downwards, about a foot over her head for perhaps the next twenty seconds. Within two min-

utes of the time Felisa started, Dr. Stelter, Alex and I observed, with our eyes only eighteen inches from the action spot, the sharp point of a piece of glass appear on the surface. Felisa took this between her thumb and forefinger and held it out to show us. It was very sharp and slightly over one half inch in length. There was no blood on the palm or the glass. There was no sign of a "hole" in the tissue of the palm.[11]

ALEX ORBITO AND MARCELO JAINAR

Dr. Alfred Stelter, a psychic researcher and author of "Psychoenergetic Phenomena" leaves us breathless:

I observed another form of psychokinesis in September, 1973—the paranormal taking out and replacement of eyeballs. Without any instruments to help in reaching behind the eyeball, healers were able to take it out completely. When I saw this done by Alex Orbito and by Marcelo Jainar, I was always very close and was accompanied by a veterinary doctor who specialized in animal eye surgery and who also had a vast knowledge of the human body.[12]

JUANITO FLORES AND JOSE MERCADO

Alfred Stelter also reports on the surgery on the "etheric" body performed by some healers, notably Juanito Flores and Jose Mercado:

The healer reaches into the air for an imaginary hypodermic needle which he places on the Bible, in order to "charge" it. Then he aims it at the patient, moves a finger as if he were giving a shot, often without touching the body, and sometimes from a distance of as much as one meter. At times this is pointed to the exposed skin and at other times through the clothes toward some specific spot on the body. Dr. Theo Locher, editor of "Swiss Bulletin for Parapsychology," wrote in May, 1973:

In February, 1972, the Italian neurologist Prof. F. Granome of Vercelli undertook an extended investigation of nine healers in the Philippines with a team of scientists and camera crews for fifteen days. Spiritual injections were applied by hand without touching the body. These injections made the seven Europeans of the team feel needles or electric shock at the particular place on their body. Three members experienced bleeding. The analysis of the blood samples, made by Medical Institute of the University of Turin, showed that *it was not human blood*. In spite of movie cameras, infrared photos and other observations of the entry point, nothing suspicious was found. The analysis of the blood running down the leg of another team member was not blood either, which the research team could not understand.

A piece of paper placed under the shirt of one of the scientists showed three small holes where the injection was made. The hands of the healer were constantly under observation of the team's cameras and never came closer than one-half meter to the patient. At one time I myself received an injection in my left lower thigh without the healer coming closer than one meter. At this treatment quite a bit of blood ran down from the entry point, and had to be wiped up several times with cotton before the bleeding could be stopped.[13]

JUAN BLANCE

Stelter has this to say of the astonishing Juan Blance:

Since February, 1971, I have often seen a fourth variant of psychokinesis under many different conditions with healer Juan Blance of Manila. He produces a psychokinetic cut on the skin. Usually he takes the index finger of an observer, forms a fist of all other fingers and thumb of this observer's hand, and with it makes jerky motions 20 or 30 cm. above the skin of the patient. A cut appears on the skin underneath, such as would be made by a razor blade, and the healer sometimes withdraws a substantial amount of blood using a glass suction cup. The blood sometimes contains tissue substances. That this psychokinetic cut made by both Blance and David Oligani is genuine, is disputed by many observers with little experience. It is said the healers secretly used sharp objects such as slivers of glass or small pieces of razor blades attached to a false thumb in order to make an opening in the skin, the cut being so light as not to be noticeable at first. The blood would then come with time, making it look like a psychokinetic cut.

Since the attention of the patient and the spectators is not usually directed to the place until the blood was slowly trickling out (often under pressure on the skin at the sides of the cut), skeptics say that the healer previously wiped the place to be opened with a cotton swab which concealed some mechanical aid and it was this item which caused the skin to open. For four years I frequently watched and studied Blance's psychokinetic cuts, both in Manila and during his visit to Germany during four weeks in January, 1974. The cut is not always done the same way. I often saw incisions appear without any contact or any previous treatment of the skin, where the skin burst open the moment the movement occurred in the air. In these cases the healer had very strong mediumistic powers. In other cases the healer apparently needed the contact with the skin, which opened after the healer placed a finger or thumb on the spot. (This recalls what may be a similar situation in the bending of metal of Uri Geller and by the British or Japanese children, sometimes without being touched, and when it is touched, the contact or stroking is so slight it could not possibly explain the bending of the metal.)

In the case of many of the incisions, I felt the movement of the fingers through the air way symbolical and the cut happened independently from it, or was there before it. . . . In February, 1975, I checked to see if the psychokinetic incisions have ionizing rays in strong measure. I used films which are used in Germany to protect people working with radioactive materials. The films, sealed in plastic film holders, were placed on the patient's skin before Blance made his incision from a distance. After his fingers moved through the air, the film was untouched at the top but the skin was cut and the film was scratched on its underside. . . . [later] a strange phenomenon happened in connection with the psychokinetic cut. The cut appeared under the bookmark hanging from the Bible (which Blance and other healers often have some person hold over the patient during the treatment) and was induced through it. Probably it was at this point that the usually controllable psychokinetic powers began to get out of control. Blance became very restless when the cuts became uncontrollable and continued to be made through the bookmark and appear where they were not supposed to appear—even on the back of the healer's hand. While he and Irene Lutz were working on the upper part of a patient's body, cuts also appeared on the hands of the assistant who was massaging the feet of the patient during the treatment! We can see here the distinct change of controlled psychokinesis to an uncontrollable form.

Two days later he [Blance] had a complete breakdown with life-endangering heart and circulation collapse. Perhaps it is due to the magnetic healing powers of Irene Lutz that he is still alive. Since the healer refused any kind of medication or admittance to a hospital, his life was in danger for several days before he was able to return to Manila.

When I visited Manila a month later on my next study trip, Blance had slowly resumed work but was still very weak. He still had scars from the psychokinetic cuts on the backs of his own hands.

Often large tumors were brought out by Blance after he had made the incision. In 1971 I watched a tumor the size of a plum come out of the hip of a Filipino patient. This tumor was not separated by any mechanical method. It really seemed to jump into the hand of the healer. I never again observed such an impressive phenomenon at Blance's.[14]

EDIVALDO

G. L. Playfair, author of *The Unknown Power*, a book on psychic surgery and the occult, decided to visit a psychic surgeon for his stomach problems. The following is his account. His awareness of two pairs of hands working inside him is most striking, as well as his physical condition after the first operation, which plainly indicates that something physical can occur in the surgery:

Edivaldo's hands seemed to find what they were looking for, the thumbs pressed down hard, and I felt a very distinct plop as they penetrated the skin and went inside. My stomach immediately felt wet all over, as if I were bleeding to death. I could feel a sort of tickling inside, but no pain at all. The most unusual sensation was a strong smell of ether, which seemed to come from my stomach area and drift upwards past my nose. . . . (After the operation) I was completely rigid all over my middle area. I had difficulty in breathing properly, and still had the sensation of having a hole in my stomach. . . . Bending to unlace my shoes proved impossible, so I had to force them off with my feet. . . . There was a bright red mark on the place where Edivaldo had pressed with his thumbs, and nearby were two bright red dots. . . . The red dots never faded and I still have them. . . . The second operation took place about five months after the first. . . . After his hands had probed around for a few moments, again I felt that plop as they went inside. . . . I felt a firm wrench in my innards—deep down, not just on the surface—and there was a slight pain, though not enough to make me yell. I had the curious sensation that there were two sets of hands at work on me; Edivaldo seemed to be doing no more than just keep his hands there while another invisible pair did the actual work.[15]

TERTE

Psychic surgery may be combined with psychic healing methods as well. Harold Sherman in his *"Wonder" Healers in the Philippines* records the healing of a crippled boy by Terte (the condition was much improved but the recovery was not total):

Terte manipulated the leg gently, examining front and back, and then said: "This is too serious. He needs magnetic healing for strength before I can operate." . . . [Later] Terte reached into a nearby open Bible and held an invisible hypodermic syringe. Danny was apparently given a shot, on the back of his left knee and on the arch of his left foot. To this, my son commented that he had felt a prickly sensation. . . .

The psychic surgeon asked his helper for a coin and was handed a copper-colored 25 centavo piece. This was placed on the back of Danny's upper leg, near the spot of the tumor. A piece of oil-soaked cotton was then put on top of the coin. I gasped as Blance lit a match and set fire to the cotton. My son was looking bored, gazing off into space as if waiting for something to happen. I couldn't believe the heat conducted into the circle of metal from the blaze would go unnoticed.

"Is it burning you?" I asked, quietly.

"Is what burning me?" he replied.

"Nothing, never mind," I answered, mystified by the whole thing.

Blance took a small tumbler, the size of a shot glass, and placed it over the coin. The fire went out instantly. As he took his finger and tapped on the top of the glass, fresh blood appeared on the skin surface, following the outline of the glass. I peered very closely as did my mother, but when this apparatus was removed, there was no cut or opening on the skin to indicate where the blood was flowing from. Neither was there a mark or redness from the heat.

Blance reached for my mother's right hand and doubled it into a fist, leaving her forefinger extended. Holding her hand within his, directly over the center of that circle of blood, he made a quick, cutting motion. Instantly, a pink slash appeared in the skin, some eight inches beneath her forefinger—about one and a half inches in length!

"My finger did that!" Mother gasped, but I barely heard her. Every nerve and muscle in my body was focused on Blance's movements. He was placing the tips of his fingers on the bloody circle and drawing them together toward the center of the cut. I saw something coming out of the incision. With his forefinger and thumb, he reached into the opening and partially withdrew a piece of hard-looking tissue. Blance halted abruptly as the mass was three-quarters out and turned to look at me, as if to say: "Do you believe it now? I'm waiting for you. Go on, take a picture!"

After my flash bulb exploded, Blance pulled the remainder of the tissue out. He held it up for me to take another picture before dropping it into a nearby waste basket. Whatever came out of my son's leg was now mingled with other unidentified traces of blood from Danny's leg. I held my breath. This was that unbelievable moment when no break or mar would remain on the skin to indicate the surgery of a second before.

To my surprise, Blance merely pinched the skin together, leaving the gash that would take two weeks to heal naturally.

"But why doesn't he close it?" I asked the assistant.

"There is too much doubt you have. Now this will be your proof," came the reply.[16]

Thus far we have seen the clearly irrational aspect

of the surgery. It surely does not conform to any sort of medical knowledge or procedure. Such aspects as the tingling, prickling sensation felt in the above case are universally common among mediums and occultists and consistently occur in conjunction with the activity of the spirits, not of doctors. In fact, that sensation is sort of a demonic theme. It occurs so regularly in clearly occult activities that when it appears in what many would call borderline areas (e.g., magnetic or pranic healing), we may fairly conclude that it is actually the same energy utilized by mediums and occultists.

RUTHLESS SURGICAL PROCEDURES

The surgeons are often ruthless in their procedures. It is as if they are saying, "It's not how you do it, but *who* does it that is important. We can cure disease and sickness that modern medicine cannot, and that is all that matters." Lourival de Freitas is better known in Europe than in his native Brazil since he does most of his healing there. The following describes an operation performed on a young girl.

> [She] was suffering from saturation of the lungs and was gradually being choked to death, being considered an inoperable case. Lourival had insisted on the operation being performed in a yacht, of all places, moored in the Bay of Guanabara some distance from the beaches of Rio de Janeiro. As the small boat swayed to and fro, Lourival plunged a pair of scissors down the girl's throat with considerable violence and began to make cutting movements—and sounds.
>
> At this point, one onlooker rushed out on deck in terror, and later refused even to discuss the affair with me, saying that even thinking about it made her feel sick.

The patient showed signs of considerable pain for a few minutes, but Lourival then picked her up by her legs and held her upside down, upon which quantities of liquid flowed out of her mouth onto the floor of the cabin. After this experience, the girl made an apparently complete recovery and was able to go out to parties and to dance, which she had been too weak to do previously.

After about a year, however, she felt signs that her old problem was returning, after which I lost touch with her. This is not the only case where cures by psychic surgery appear to have been only temporary."[17]

Antonio Sales has the same spirit guide that Arigo had ("Dr. Fritz") and is also noted for his eye operations. However, he performs on other parts of the body just as ruthlessly as Arigo did on the eyes.

Another witness had described to me how Sales operated on the throat of a girl apparently suffering from tonsillitis. "He thrust a pair of scissors into her mouth and started cutting away, telling the girl not to worry because everything was sterilized. I noticed a smell of ether around the place, but saw no sign of anybody sterilizing anything at all. Some blood came out of the girl's mouth, but very little, and two hours later she was eating a huge steak."

The same girl had been told to take massive doses of antibiotics, but had found no chemist willing to make up the prescription. She soon became ill with a high fever, and only after her desperate family had persuaded a nervous family doctor to rewrite the prescription was she able to get hold of the antibiotics. These, I was told, cured her.[18]

Materialization Phenomena

The strange smells that accompany psychic surgery appear to be related to the process of mate-

rialization of phenomena during the surgery and indicate that the blood, tissues, tumors, and so forth,
in many cases are demonically apported from
somewhere else and materialized during the
surgery for, essentially, psychological impact.

Dr. Stelter describes the activity of several healers
in his discussion on materialization phenomena during surgery:

> This subject has been one of my main interests dur-
> ing the many visits to observe the Filipino healers. I
> share the opinion of Dr. Andrija Puharich that if sci-
> ence could really uncover the processes involved in
> materialization and dematerialization, much of
> modern science would be due for some substantial
> revisions and expansion.
>
> Perhaps the easiest materialization to describe
> and to visualize is its practice by Josefina Sison and
> others in making surgical cotton disappear and
> reappear on the surface of the patient's body. The
> cotton, often moistened with consecrated coconut
> oil, is formed into a tight wad and seemingly pressed
> into and through the skin, into the patient's chest,
> abdomen, head, arm or leg; and when she opens
> her hand, the cotton is gone. Sometimes she will
> leave the cotton in place and other times she may
> immediately—or on the next visit—seemingly re-
> move the cotton. If the cotton is removed on a sub-
> sequent visit, it is often red with blood, while newly
> inserted cotton comes out as white as it went in.
>
> I am not so naive that I am unable to spot trickery. I
> have observed this materialization by Josefina and
> other healers many hundreds of times, under all
> kinds of conditions. Dr. Hiram Ramos and other
> companions of mine have repeatedly asked Josefina
> to open her hands before starting to "stuff" the cotton
> and after it had disappeared. We ourselves have
> handed her the cotton. One of the most revealing
> investigations was made by my colleague Prof. Dr.
> Werner Schiebeler who filmed this action in high-

intensity lighting with 16mm color film. Examination frame by frame shows the cotton actually disappearing between her fingers and it does not appear to physically pass through the patient's skin. . . .

Even though the literature of the last 100 years is replete with well-documented cases of materialization and dematerialization, one's mind still tends to reject what his eyes are seeing. Only after long experience of the phenomena does it become any more credible. In the case of the "cotton-stuffing" activity, I personally feel that one of the most convincing incidents is to see a healer remove what is apparently blood-soaked cotton from a patient, cotton which had been put into that patient several days earlier by another healer, whose identity is immediately sensed by the healer who is removing the cotton. Where was the cotton in the interval between its "insertion" and its "removal?" Was it in a state of fine material structure in the bioplasmic body of the patient or was it in the astral level, outside of our space-time framework?

The statement made by Harold Sherman in 1966 to the effect that Filipino healers can open the human body is basically correct. In my nine months in the Philippines watching the work of the healers day after day, I had a few rare opportunities to see truly sensational dematerialization of body tissue of patients.

In February, 1971, Tony Agpaoa dematerialized flesh of a 38-year-old patient to expose the leg bone which, broken 16 years previously, had not knitted properly. I saw clearly and took photos of the broken ends of the bone. There was quite a flow of blood but after the "operation" the leg looked the same as it had before, since none of the bloody tissue remained. A photo taken by me proved that I had not been hypotized and had not hallucinated, but had observed correctly. (A report some time later indicated that the leg had not been healed.)

When Blance treats a patient with a skin disease,

he sometimes seems to be pulling through the skin, spindle-like pieces of yellow substance that looks like very small grass blades. However, the texture is more like wax. I have seen this phenomenon many times under conditions where fraud was absolutely impossible.

For example, in Frankfurt, Germany, Blance was treating a long line of patients one after another as their turns came. Since they had the normal gamut of illnesses he never knew which ailment he would be treating next. A friend of mine suffering from shingles, climbed onto the table and Blance, with his eyes closed and apparently in deep concentration, ran his hands over my friend's body. When he found the affected area, he proceeded to "extract" the above described "grass blades." After six visits in a few days, the shingles had disappeared.

In September, 1973, I saw healer Romy Bugarin, accompanied by a medical doctor, perform what was to me a sensational abdominal "operation" on a Filipino woman medical doctor. Romy entered the body through the abdomen, separated the organs, and lifted some organs outside the body cavity. When Romy closed the body there was some tissue left outside and considerable bloodlike liquid.

These and other "operations" I have witnessed in the Philippines are outstanding, but it appears that this level of mediumistic work cannot be performed in the environment of a scientific laboratory in Europe or the U.S.A.[19]

That most unusual account of several incidents raises many questions. What are the reasons behind such uses of cotton? How could Agpaoa dematerialize the flesh of a patient's leg and then not heal the bone? Why are those phenomena not reproducible in a laboratory setting? As we shall see later, the answers lie in the realm of a "faith" factor, which is both necessary during the operation and purposely induced in the patient.

Spiritist Dr. Ary Lex, a distinguished Brazilian surgeon and member of several professional organizations, describes Arigo's uncanny power to stop the flow of blood on command and to remove the eye from its socket:

> . . . the way Arigo would simply turn his back on the patient in the middle of an operation, the way he would just touch some blood flowing from an eye and it would stop at once, or the way he would pull an eye right out of its socket without causing a trace of pain.[20]

In a final example of the phenomena of pychic surgery, Playfair describes a case of eye removal by Arigo and his prescription methods, which demonstrate the hostility against modern medicine so evident in occult healing:

> Next came one of Arigo's traditional specialities; the ablation or removal of a pterygium from a woman's eye. This was done with an ordinary pair of nail scissors, and when blood began to trickle from the eye, Arigo simply dabbed at it with cotton wool and told it to stop, which it did. I have also seen this on film, and Dr. Lex assures me that he knows of no way in which the amount of blood he saw can normally be made to coagulate so quickly.
>
> What really shook Dr. Lex (and me, while watching Rizzini's film), was the incredible roughness, at times amounting to violence of Arigo's surgical techniques. He would pick up his knife, which looked like an ordinary table knife, and simply shove it under the eyeball, sometimes taking his hand away and letting it hang there. The patient would appear apprehensive, though showing no trace of any pain. Worst of all was Arigo's disconcerting habit of appearing to take little interest in what he was doing, frequently looking over his shoulder while poking around with somebody's eyeball half out of its socket.

An important point regarding Dr. Lex's testimony is that he is himself an active Spiritist of more than 25 years' standing, and a frequent speaker of the Sao Paulo Spiritist Federation, where a favourite theme of his is the need to expose fraudulent mediums who only serve to discredit the movement. He is not a man one can describe as credulous, for he has examined several other alleged medium healers and remained unimpressed by any of them. He is also sharply critical of Arigo's prescriptions, some of which he was able to examine on the spot.

"They were absolutely ridiculous," he told me. "Some of them were for obsolete medicines which were only still being made because he prescribed them." He mentioned one, known in Brazil as Kanamicina, which he considered not only obsolete but actually dangerous. He also told me that Arigo would prescribe alarmingly large quantities of medicines, which quite apart from their possible side effects were extremely expensive. He estimated the cost of one prescription he saw as equal to about one hundred U.S. dollars.[21]

Psychic Surgery and Shamanism

Although many people think psychic surgery is "something new," it is in fact something very old. It seems to have simply been modified for modern Western consumption. If we study the techniques of shaman healers, we find many parallels to psychic surgery (see Mircea Eliade's *Shamanism: Archaic Techniques of Ecstasy* and Michael Harner's *Hallucinogens and Shamanism*.[22] Shamanism is more primitive and ritualistic than psychic surgery, but in healing they represent a similar phenomenon, with certain aspects changed in order to accommodate the particular culture. Eliade, who has studied shamanistic cultures worldwide, states: "As everywhere else, the essential and strictly personal function of the South American Shaman remains healing."[23]

The shaman always diagnoses by help of the spirits. In Central and North Asia, "Before undertaking a cure the shaman enters into contact with his spirits to learn the cause of the illness."[24] In North and South America, "In cases of illness brought on by the introduction of a harmful magical object, it is always by virtue of his ecstatic [trance] capacities, and not by any reasoning in the realm of secular science, that the shaman is able to diagnose the case; he commands a number of helping spirits who seek the cause of the illness for him, and the seance necessarily implies summoning up these spirits."[25] "The shaman sometimes loses himself in meditation and talks *sotto voce:* he is conversing with his *damagomi*, his 'powers' (helping spirits), to discover the cause of the illness. For it is really the *damagomi* that make the diagnosis."[26] Anthropologist Kensinger discusses the process among natives of the upper Amazon:

> A shaman is consulted. He reviews the history of the case and then consults his spirit familiars about the cause of the illness, normally an intrusive object or spirit which he then removes from the patient with a small quantity of muka dau, "bitter medicine" which resides in the shaman's body, and which must then be removed from the patient by the herbalist's sweet medicine. It is only when these procedures fail to produce the desired cure that the shaman resorts to ayahuasca [a hallucinogenic drug]. A special drinking session is called, during which the shaman consults with spirits outside his normal sphere of influence, who inform him of the cause of the illness, or a new chant which should be used along with sucking

or massage, or the kind of sweet medicine to request from the herbalist, or that the illness is incurable.[27]

Eliade finds that "the shamanistic trance forms part of the cure. . . . it is always by his ecstasy that he finds the exact cause of the illness and learns the best treatment. The trance sometimes ends in the shaman's 'possession' by his familiar spirits."[28]

In psychic surgery, after completion of the operation, the surgeon may emphasize the importance of a correct spiritual discipline (usually spiritistic) as necessary for ongoing health. That is evident in shamanism, since "the recovery of physical health is closely dependent upon restoring the balance of spiritual forces, for it is often the case that the illness is due to a neglect or an omission in respect to the infernal powers [spirits], which also belong to the sphere of the sacred."[29]

The parallels between psychic surgery and shamanism are evident. Some shamans even perform "modern" psychic surgery:

> The Chukchee shamans also know another classic method of cure: suction. After performing it, they display the cause of the illness—an insect, a pebble, a thorn, or similar objects. Often they undertake an "operation" that still preserves all its shamanic character. With a ritual knife, duly "heated" by certain magical exercises, the shaman professes to open the patient's body to examine his internal organs and remove the cause of the illness. Bogoras even witnessed an "operation" of this kind. A boy of fourteen lay naked on the ground, and his mother, a celebrated shamaness, opened his abdomen; the blood and the gaping flesh were visible; the shamaness thrust her hand deep into the wound. During all this time the shamaness felt as if she were on fire and constantly drank water. A few moments later

the wound had closed, and Bogoras could detect no trace of it.

Another shaman, after drumming for a long time to "heat" his body and his knife to the point at which, he said, the cuts would not be felt, opened his own abdomen. Such feats are frequent throughout North Asia, and they are connected with the "mastery over fire," for the same shamans who gash their bodies are able to swallow burning coals and to touch white-hot iron. The majority of these "tricks" are performed in broad daylight.[30]

It is relevant that the introductory process required to become a shaman is repeated in the initiation of at least some psychic surgeons. (We might also note that many leaders or founders of modern-day cults underwent essentially shamanistic initiations in the course of their own spiritual quest.) Shaman initiation involves periods of temporary unconsciousness, insanity, possession, and battles with the spirits, culminating in eventual victory and the bestowal of psychic and healing powers by the spirits.

Psychic surgeon Edivaldo describes his own first successful healing and introduction to psychic surgery, essentially a shaman initiation. In 1962 he went to visit a neighbor who had gone temporarily insane:

> I went to sit with her while they fetched a doctor. When we were alone together I suddenly went mad myself for about an hour. I was completely unconscious; a spirit took me over and I became violent. When I recovered there were broken things all over the place, but the woman had got better.[31]

He subsequently had recurring possessions and healings, was trained by a local spiritist center, and became a psychic surgeon. Since that first episode, he has performed some 65,000 healings and operations.[32]

SPIRIT SELECTION

Even the modern healer's introduction to psychic healing or surgery is shamanist. As a shaman is often chosen directly for the job *by the spirits*, so is the modern healer. The spirits are aggressive and, if given the opportunity, will take the initiative. It is also true that in the case of modern and shamanist healers, one does not need to be chosen but may choose involvement. If that is the case, however, the initiate nearly always requires the personal assistance of an accomplished healer.

Although often there is a direct choosing (more common to the shaman and surgeon than the psychic healer), a spirit does not have to appear visibly to manipulate a person into the field of psychic healing. The spirits have a wide variety of subtle methods and techniques, both to get the attention and then the allegiance of those for whom they have plans. In modern cultures where spirit contact is still viewed with suspicion, it is those methods and not the shamanist approach that are apparent. That subtle initiative of the spirits is indicated by Sally Hammond, a prize-winning reporter for the *New York Post*, in her extensive questionnaire survey of 150 British healers: "The most striking aspect of their replies was the fact that so many had astonishing and sometimes eerie experiences that led them into the field of healing."[33]

Direct choice by the spirits may occur as a result of a history of occultism in the family, even to four generations. Today that generational transmission is not well recognized, but it has been demonstrated that one person's active occult involvement may condemn his children, and their children, to the special attentions of the spirit world, as if they are specially marked in some way.[34] However, being chosen is not always a prerequisite. There are just as many cases of persons' becoming healers, even surgeons, on their own—provided they undergo the necessary "training" course.

THE TRANCE STATE AND PSYCHIC SURGERY

Occult development involves breaking down the rational and normal way of relating to the world. Linear time and normal consciousness are barriers to developing psychic healing or surgery talents, or any other form of occult practice. Carlos Castanada could not become a sorcerer apart from shattering his Western view of reality, and hallucinogenic drugs were his primary means. For many people, Eastern meditation, the sensory deprivation tank, or yoga and hypnosis, are just as effective. The important factor is the attaining of new states of perception— altered or expanded consciousness, non-ordinary states of reality. That "new consciousness" is the key that causes nearly every occult-Eastern system to "work," be it Hinduism, TM, Yoga, Zen, est, magic, Buddhism, or any other form of mysticism. Gary K. North states: "It is almost as if Western rationalists were surrounded by some sort of negative aura that in some way hampers the activities of the demonic control agents. This, in fact, is precisely what old Don Juan told Castanada: 'The everyday activities of Westerners serve as shields against the powers of the spirit world. The barrier can seemingly work in an offensive fashion as well as defensively.' "[35]

The psychic surgeon cannot operate except in an altered state of consciousness (trance). Psychic healers *usually* require altered states to heal. Psychic diagnosticians like Cayce and Peterson must also be in a trance state, and so it goes.

The level of ASC (altered states of consciousness) varies with the psychic power of the person and the difficulty of the task. Arigo says, "When a case is simple, I can diagnose and prescribe without going into a trance, since Dr. Fritz guides me. But for complex cases (e.g., surgery) I must enter a trance and call on Dr. Fritz directly."[36] The fact that some forms of psychic healing are done in a normal state shows ASC's are not vital to the process, although they are often preferred by the spirits. And all healers do practice entering ASC's (e.g., in meditation) whether or not they are used during the healing.

Altered states of consciousness are a necessary part of occult development for two reasons: first, to facilitate the "psychic vampirism" that drains human energy to help in the healing; and second, for more effective control over the healer, allowing the spirit to work through him more easily. Distant healing would not necessarily need ASC's because the spirit would be utilizing its own power or an energy source in the vicinity of the patient. As we have seen, vampirized energy, or at least demonic control, is most always perceived by a tingling sensation and is found in all forms of occult healing. Some advice for developing mediums is as follows (note there is no mention of "spirits"):

> Then make yourself negative, and ask the Spiritual Power to come and help and assist you in your process of cure. Make yourself a *channel* for it. You will feel tingling sensations in your arms and the patient will feel them in his body. This is the beginning of the process.[37]

The deliberate cultivation of ASC's should perhaps be viewed as a neurosis that requires therapy instead of the updated view of "expanding one's consciousness." Man was not made to function properly, let alone safely, in those altered states any more than with a high fever. We are not created with the equipment necessary to handle or discern them efficiently, much less wisely. When we consider the fact that the psychic realm is not neutral but populated with deceptive spirits (as occultists are aware), it becomes absurd to think man can achieve anything good by contact with it.

There is one guaranteed result: a severe cost factor—borne out by the fact that the history of occultism is littered with human tragedy. The fact that the way in which we were created—with the normal functioning of the mind's acting as a barrier against the intrusion of the spirit world—tells us that entering other states is abnormal. (Today it is defined as being "enlightened.") In some cases normal consciousness does not act as a barrier, but that is due to the hereditary predisposition from familial (historical) involvement in occultism. Even here, though, a deliberate refusal to allow further contact is usually enough to keep future contacts from coming, though there may be a "test of wills." Give in or actively seek contact, and it's a whole new ball game. Once the door is opened, it can be nearly impossible to close, and the only effective deliverance is through responsible Christian counseling.[38]

If we examine Christian healing, on the other hand, we discover that it is *never* achieved via ASC's, nor is there mediumistic exhaustion afterwards, because there is no need to drain energy from the healer, as the spirits claim to do.[39] God does the healing.

SPIRIT ACCOMMODATION

In examining the history of the occult, we find that spiritistic manifestations seem to accommodate themselves to a particular time or culture. That is true of some UFO's,[40] obviously, and other occult phenomena, as well as psychic surgery. The forces behind the manifestations, in order to make contact easier, adapt themselves to the world view and expectations of the contemporary people. That is true individually and culturally. We remember that Edgar Cayce and Ross Peterson did not like the idea of "spirit contact"; therefore the manifestations were claimed to be of the unconscious or "higher self." The spirits accommodated themselves to the belief structures of their contacts.

In the case of psychic surgery, before Americans came to Brazil and the Philippines in large numbers, the psychic surgery was markedly different. Because of the primitive culture, it was essentially shamanistic in method, that is, there was no "blood and guts"; diseases were said to have been caused directly by spirits and black magic. But the removal of "witchcraft items" (crystals and bamboo shoots believed to cause sickness and death by hexing) from the bodies of the educated Americans would have no meaning for them. They would expect to see what *their* culture defines as the cause of illness—tumors or diseased tissue, for example. And after all, since blood always accompanies surgery, blood must be present as well. And thus, as soon as Americans arrived, they saw just what they expected.

The apostle Paul's desire to be all things to all people is effectively imitated by Satan as well (1 Corinthians 9:22):

> Whereas extracting a 'witchcraft item' such as coconut fiber from the abdomen of a woman from Chicago, London or Zurich would have been repulsive and non-productive psychologically, the appearance of *blood and tissue* was readily accommodated by the belief system of such a patient.

Some of the healers found this new development a

bit disconcerting. Tony Agpaoa in recalling this period is quoted in a purported "conversation" with his "protector" or guiding entity:

"But let there be no blood," murmered Tony.

"Without blood to show," came the *voice*, "even those completely healed will not believe."

"Well, perhaps, not so *much* blood. The sight and smell of it sickens me," said Tony.

"It sickens me, too, but it is also *proof* that they might *believe*."[41]

Dr. Hans Naegeli-Osjord also noted the "switch-over":

It seems that during the first fifty years (since 1903) of divine services of the Philippine spiritualists, only "magnetic" (no so-called "bloody") healings took place. However, shortly before 1950 we find that Terte, Gonzales, Sarmiento, and others in rural— almost archaic—regions began to penetrate the body with what then became known by the term "psychic surgery."[42]

The psychological importance of visible blood, as well as the display of the removed objects, are central to psychic surgery. In shamanism that is also evident, although slightly altered because shaman tribesmen would not understand Western surgical techniques or procedures:

After finding the cause of the illness, the shaman begins the cure. Except in cases of soul loss, treatment consists in extracting the "trouble" or in sucking blood. By suction, the shaman draws out with his teeth a small object "like a bit of black or white thread, sometimes like a nail paring." An Achomawi told De Angulo: "I don't believe those things come out of the sick man's body. The shaman always has them in his mouth before he starts the treatment. But he draws the sickness into them, he uses them to catch the poison. Otherwise, how could he catch it?"

Some shamans suck the blood directly. A shaman explained how he went about it: "It is black blood, it is bad blood. First, I spit it into my hands to see if the sickness is really in it. Then I hear my damagomi [spirits] quarreling. They all want me to give them something to drink. They have worked well for me. They have helped me. Now they are all hot. They're thirsty. They want to drink. They want to drink blood. . . ." If he does not give them blood, the damagomi rush wildly about and protest clamorously. "Then I drink blood. I swallow it. I give it to them. And that quiets them. That calms them. That refreshes them. . . ."

According to De Angulo's observations, the "bad blood" is not sucked from the patient's body; it is "the product of a hemorrhagic extravasation, of hysterical origin, in the shaman's stomach." And in fact the shaman is extremely tired at the end of a seance and, after drinking two or three quarts of water, "falls into a heavy sleep."

However this may be, sucking blood appears to be an aberrant form of shamanic healing. It will be recalled that some Siberian shamans likewise drink the blood of the sacrificed animals and claim that it is really their helping spirits that demand and drink it. This extremely complex rite, based on the sacred value of hot blood, is "shamanic" only secondarily and through coalescence with other rites belonging to different magico-religious complexes.

If the case is one of poisoning by another shaman, the healer, after sucking the skin for a long time, seizes the magical object with his teeth and displays it. Sometimes the poisoner is among the audience, and the shaman returns the "object" to him: "There is your damagomi, I don't want to keep it for myself!"[43]

Psychic diagnosis, healing, and surgery, as the reader may well have apprehended by this time, represent different degrees of the same phenomenon. What we have been talking about is demonic activity and the miracles performed by the nether powers for their own purposes. Where the miracles are simple the explanations are simple; where they become more heroic, the explanations are still simple. The enemy is a spirit, and a powerful spirit. Rather like any other entertainer, he accommodates his particular audience, opting for the most remarkable demonstrations when the situation calls for them.

Fascinating as all psychic surgery is, we find it to be a step backward rather than an advance in medical science. Psychic researchers and parapsychologists claim that we are entering a new era of healing by means of the astonishing reports above. But in reality the psychic surgeon is a combination of shaman and spiritist. The psychic surgeon represents a kind of return to primitivism and occult bondage of a savage kind.

NOTES

1. Guy L. Playfair, The Unknown Power, p. 168. Copyright 1975 by Simon & Schuster. Used by permission.
2. See for example George W. Meek, ed., Healers and the Healing Process, chapters 3, 6-12, especially pp. 64-77. Copyright 1977 by the Theosophical Publishing House. Used by permission.
3. Playfair, p. 136.
4. Gary K. North, None Dare Call It Witchcraft, p. 165.
5. George W. Meek, "The Healers in Brazil, England, U.S.A. and U.S.S.R.," in Meek, pp. 62-63.
6. Stanley Krippner and Alberto Villoldo, The Realms of Healing, pp. 7-8. Copyright 1976. Reprinted through the courtesy of Celestial Arts Publishing Company, Millbrae, California.

7. From *Arigo: Surgeon of the Rusty Knife* by John G. Fuller, (Thomas Y. Crowell Co. Copyright © 1974 by John G. Fuller. Reprinted by permission of Harper & Row Publishers, Inc.), pp. 18-19.
8. Andruja Puharich, "Paranormal Healing in Brazil—Arigo," in Meek, pp. 42-43.
9. Playfair, pp. 128-29.
10. Fuller, p. 203.
11. Meek, "The Healers," in Meek, pp. 63-64.
12. Alfred Stelter, "Psychoenergetic Phenomena," in Meek, p. 72.
13. Ibid., pp. 72-73.
14. Ibid., pp. 73-75.
15. Playfair, pp. 160-63.
16. Harold Sherman, *Wonder Healers of the Philippines*, pp. 272-75. Copyright 1974 by DeVorss & Company. Used by permission.
17. Playfair, p. 136.
18. Ibid., p. 132.
19. Stelter, in Meek, pp. 76-77.
20. Playfair, pp. 121-22.
21. Ibid., pp. 122-23.
22. Mircea Eliade, *Shamanism: Archaic Techniques of Ecstasy*, pp. 215-58, 300-308, 326-32. Copyright 1972. Reprinted by permission of Princeton University Press.
23. Ibid., p. 326.
24. Ibid., p. 227.
25. Ibid., pp. 300-301.
26. Ibid., p. 305.
27. Kenneth M. Kensinger, "Banisteriopsis Usage Among the Peruvian Cashinahua," in Michael Harner, ed., *Hallucinogens and Shamanism*, p. 14.
28. Eliade, p. 328.
29. Ibid., p. 216.
30. Ibid.

31. Playfair, pp. 166-67.
32. Ibid., p. 167.
33. Sally Hammond, "What the Healers Say: A Survey of Healers in Britain," p. 13.
34. See Kurt Koch, *Christian Counseling and Occultism*, p. 186.
35. North, pp. 161-62.
36. Fuller, p. 152.
37. Hereward Carrington, *Your Psychic Powers and How to Develop Them*, p. 163.
38. Puharich, "Paranormal Healing in Brazil—Arigo," in Meek, p. 38.
39. Kurt Koch, *Christian Counseling and Occultism;* Kurt Koch, *Occult Bondage and Deliverance.*
40. John Weldon and Zola Levitt, *Encounters with UFOs,* chapter 2.
41. George W. Meek and David Hoy, "Deception and Sleight-of-Hand," in Meek, p. 100.
42. Hans Naegeli-Osjord, "Psychiatric and Psychological Considerations," in Meek, p. 81.
43. Eliade, pp. 307-8.

7

Spirit Powers at Work: An Analysis

It should be clear by now that we have really examined only a single subject—the occult—though it may divide itself into several medical areas. We have found that those who diagnose, those who heal, and those who operate surgically depend on the same sources, enter the same trances, and contact the same spirits. From this point on we shall use the term *psychic healing* in a general sense to cover the entire spectrum of occult medicine.

UNITY OF THE SPIRITISTIC HYPOTHESIS

It is important for us to realize that these three areas (diagnosis, healing, surgery) represent an essential unity, one phenomenon, with one source and one purpose. (See chart.)

Psychic Jeffrey Mishlove relates an incident in *Roots of Consciousness* that helps indicate that unity. An acquaintance of his had recently seen a movie on psychic surgery and became so fascinated that he went to the Philippines and joined a team of psychic surgeons. In the ensuing years he received the guidance of spirits speaking through mediums:

Topic	Shamanism	Psychic Surgery	Psychic or "Spiritual" Healing
Hereditary Transference	Yes	Yes	Yes
ASC	Yes—via hallucinogens/ spirits	Yes—via spiritist trance	Yes—via meditation/at-tunement, etc.
Methods	Spirits	Spirits	Spirits ("higher self," etc.)
Can healing be nonorganic?	Yes	Yes	Yes, (Mishlove, p. 140)
Cultural Accommodation	Yes	Yes	Yes
Mediumistic exhaustion	Yes	Yes	Yes
Materialization and apport phenomena	Yes	Yes	NA
Body may become clairvoyantly seen as if X-ray machine were in use	Yes	Yes	Yes
Psychic phenomena in healer from childhood on	Yes	Yes	Yes
Chosen for the work by spirits	Yes	Yes	Yes
Exhaustive knowledge of modern pharmacology	Not needed or expected	Yes	Yes
Anesthesia by nonphysical or nonmedical means	Yes	Yes	NA
World view	Occult	Occult	Occult

*NA=Not applicable.

Spiritism	Mesmerism	Psychic Diagnosis	Christian Healing
Yes	Yes	Yes	No
Yes—via trance	Yes—of patient	Yes—via several methods	No
Spirits	Spirits suspect in some cases	Spirits psychometry, etc.	God
Yes	?	NA*	No
Yes	?	Yes	No
Yes	Yes (Koch, Christian Counseling and Occultism, p. 123)	?	No
Yes	NA	NA	No
Yes	Yes	Yes	No
Yes	?	Yes	No
Yes	?	Yes	No
Yes, when occasion demands	NA	Yes	No
NA	NA	NA	No
Occult	Occult	Occult	Biblical

At first he was shown magnetic healing or the "laying on the hands." He was asked to practice this simple form of healing extensively and told he would become more adept through practice. The *espiritistas* believe that this form of healing is just as effective, although perhaps slower, than the more dramatic psychic surgery.

In fact, in their opinion, the surgical "gift" is simply a temporary tool which is being used by the spirit primarily in order to reach people who need to see phenomena. Often the psychic surgeons will materialize something like a piece of plastic or a tobacco leaf and claim that this was the embodiment of evil thoughts within the patient—which perhaps had been planted there as a result of a psychic attack. The object did not exist within that person before the operation, yet it often seems that it could not have been produced by sleight of hand either! Voeks, who eventually received the gift of performing the surgical operations, explains them in the following manner:

It is simply using the power of the source that you have prayed for and asked for, through your hands being a focal point.

When the hands are applied and I begin to knead the skin, I can say that the skin opens because I see it through my own visual process. However, I lose feeling in my hands up to about my elbows. They call this over there about a 10% trance. The hands do not actually go deeply into the body, but rather the afflicted area comes to the hand, as though the hand were a magnet. . . . Individual cells are separated and not severed, so you have no cell damage. The healer's hand then acts as a maintaining force to hold the skin apart and bring it together.

In my first operations I was as startled as the people who were watching. . . . I cannot control this. It is something that happens.

After Voeks had learned this skill, he operated on

his own grandmother who visited the Philippines. . . . It is his contention that the tools of psychic healing and psychic surgery are just one small part of the larger spiritualist movement in the Philippines.

Interestingly enough, several Americans who have been to the Philippines and travelled on missions have now organized a Christian spiritualist church in San Francisco based on the spirit contact which originated for them in the Philippines. Although they are not allowed to practice psychic surgery in this country, they do engage in other forms of healing when they feel they have the power and when there is the need for it.[1]

Mishlove, the first person ever to receive a doctoral degree in occultism, notes that there are thousands of such groups around the US today.

SEMANTIC DISGUISES USED

The common factor behind all psychic healing is apparently the spirit world, whether or not it is directly acknowledged or perceived. The spirits work individually and culturally, and they will not acknowledge themselves as spirits if the contact is not comfortable with the idea. Although they will often slowly condition him to accept the spirits as spirits, usually they will operate behind, or in the guise of, a variety of "progressive" concepts—the "higher self," Christ Consciousness, inner divinity, Akashic records, cosmic forces, expanded consciousness, the creative field, psychic energy, and so forth. When demons do directly appear, it is inevitably in the service of benevolence—good angels, ascended masters, "higher beings," the luminous ones, and so forth. Obviously no demon prefers to reveal his true nature. However, despite the attempts at camouflage, the demonic presence is still apparent. Meek states:

Any study of healers immediately brings the investigator face to face with the concept that spirit intelligences (variously referred to as guides, controls, or protectors) are working through the minds of healers to supply information of which the healer himself has no conscious knowledge.[2]

In an article entitled "What the Healers Say: A Survey of [150] Healers in Britain," reported in *Psychic* magazine, July 1973, the prevalence of sundry spirits was noted again and again by the practitioners. The following table gives a sample of the variety of spirit guises reported by psychic healers today:

Spirit Doctors
Arigo ("Dr. Fritz") and all psychic surgeons
George Chapman ("Dr. Lang")
Harold Plume ("Dr. Hoo Fang")
Henry Mandell
William Brown
Mary Rogers

Spirit Guides, Angels, The Holy Spirit, Higher Beings, Luminous Ones, Others
The Worralls
Rolling Thunder
Harry Edwards
Ronald Beesley
Eileen Roberts
Roslyn Winsky
Rosalyn Bruyere

The Unconscious, Higher Self, "God," Forces, Akashic Records, Psychic Energy, Others
Edgar Cayce
Ross Peterson
Dr. Lawrence LeShan
Dr. Christopher Woodward
Gwen Murray
"Mr. A"

Significantly, some researchers recognize that claims to healing power from the unconscious, a universal field of energy, or a higher self, are really just the same spirit healing. Parapsychologist and physician Hans Naegeli-Osjord states: "The healer attains the spiritual union, the *unio mystica* [i.e, possession] with a spirit-protector, who is a saint of the church, or the creative cosmic field of force, the "high self" of the Kahuna philosophy."[3]

Similarly, those who claim their healing power comes from psychic abilities or some other source, and not from spirits, may also claim that they can sense the presence of spirit entities while healing.[4]

It is also important to understand that healers who start out with the help of spirit guides and are consciously aware of their presence during healing may progress to the point where there is no more awareness of their presence unless the spirits wish to be recognized. In other words, there is a progressive desensitization to spirit influence. That was true for medium Harry Edwards. Even if a healer believes no spirits are present, his healing powers may well still emanate from spirits.[5] In fact, we would *expect* the spirits to keep their presence hidden in cases where it is advantageous to do so. It is to the spirits' advantage to support the fiction of "powers of the mind," universal consciousness, and so on. Camouflage promotes the idea that anyone can make contact with those "natural" areas of influence if he will attune himself through proper psychic development. That is the view presented in Amy Wallace and Bill Henkins's *The Psychic Healing Book*. Thus demons can easily work through people who are not comfortable with the idea of spiritism.

If the biblical view of man as a nonsupernatural being is correct, then all genuinely supernatural healing must come from one of two sources: God or

Satan. What most people do not appreciate is that Satan rarely shows his true face, and he effectively operates under the good name of "true spirituality" (2 Corinthians 11:14). Hence the clear majority of occult healers claim their gift of "spiritual healing" comes from God.

One might naturally ask, however, If the mind can significantly influence the body (as in placebo effects), then why not the environment, as in psychokinesis or psychic healing? The answer is that mind and body exist in a relationship that is already connected (united within a single organism). Hence it is not surprising that one part (the mind, belief) can sometimes affect the other part (physical). But the mind is *not* connected to the environment or to other people in that manner. Indeed it is not connected at all. Also, to psychologically produce great changes in the body takes a long time (e.g., developing ulcers). A psychic healing would require infinitely greater mental energy than exists in the human mind alone. That is why no matter how hard we mentally concentrate on something, attempting to move it, it just stays there.

Of course, the central premise of psychic healing, occultism in general, and Eastern religions is monism, which denies Christian dualism and the creature-Creator distinction. In those philosophies all *is* one; the mind is divine. Thus the mind (united within a single organism) can influence the environment, even thousands of miles away. Monistic philosophies are thus excellent covers (spiritual red herrings) for demonic workings. If all is one and divine, *all* manifestations of power are godly. The mind is divine and potentially omnipotent.

It is important to note here that the prevailing view of the supposedly neutral Akashic records, psychic power, universal mind, and so on is that they are seen as virtual manifestations of God. In other words, once tapped, *they* contain everything a person could ever need for fulfillment, spiritual or otherwise. In effect that is a most subtle form of idolatry. For example, Mr. A. says of the "ring," the source of his power: "Here all wisdom and knowledge are stored."[6] In contrast, Colossians 2:3 says of *Christ*, "In whom are hidden all the treasures of wisdom and knowledge." The "neutral" psychic concepts usurp God's glory and give it to men, while leading them into the camp of His enemy.

Unless they are fraudulent, all forms of psychic healing are developed by occult methods. Kurt Koch states that the so-called spiritual healers of our age utilize powers that are "almost without exception of a mediumistic nature."[7] Psychic healers are themselves in agreement: Amy Wallace and Bill Henkin state in *The Psychic Healing Book*, "Psychic abilities and healing abilities are so closely related that there's almost no point in making any distinction between them."[8] We would do well to cite Hans Holtzer again:

> Psychic healing, of course, is in itself part of the occult sciences; the majority of mediums, whether professional or amateur, have some healing gift and are able to perform healings—largely because the force that makes healings possible is the same force that makes psychic phenomena in general possible. It may be utilized to make communications between the so-called dead and the living available to those seeking them, or it may be used in one of several ways as the driving power behind physical phenomena, clairvoyance, psychometry, and the entire range of ESP phenomena. The choice is the user's.[9]

In fact, the relationship is so close that one can find actual seance phenomena occurring in psychic healing. Olga Worrall produces an ectoplasmic mist that sometimes emanates from her hands. Her biographer, Edwina Cerutli, described it as "an almost colorless, thin kind of vapory stuff that floated like smoke from the absolutely non-existent space between Olga's hand and Keith's body."[10] Worrall even calls it ectoplasm and has produced it in more solid form on numerous occasions in other psychic experiments.[11] (That ectoplasmic manifestations also occur in psychic surgery, as reported by Dr. Stelter,[12] is not surprising since psychic surgery is so obviously mediumistic.)

In essence, *psychic healers are mediums.* The strong, sickening odor reportedly present in occult rituals, seances, UFO sightings, and the like, occurs as well during psychic surgery, although the spirits can also produce perfume when it suits their purpose. George Allen reported that while he was being healed by Agpaoa, "Each time an incision was made there was a strong odor like something spoiled. I don't think my blood stinks."[13]

Such phenomena appear to be associated with what UFO authority John Keel calls a transmogrification process—that is, the odor is a by-product of the materialization. The fact that the odor occurs in surgery lends credence to the idea of materialization. In other words the blood, tissue "tumors," and so forth, are *materialized* for effect and are usually not part of the person.

In animist cultures, which believe in a preponderance of demonic activity, many cures of the shaman, or witchdoctor, work *because the healers are mediums and the people are animists* (i.e., open to and sympathetic with the occult) *not* because the prescribed treatment is organically effective (frog brains cannot stop and localize for extraction the circulation of cobra venom in the blood). Cures happen because of demonic reciprocation or the "Dieri effect" (see 1 Corinthians 10:20). In the Dieri tribe, the spirits beach whales for food and keep watch on the movements of enemy tribes—in return for worship.[14]

In many modern cases, particularly in spiritist societies (Brazil, the Philippines, others) the same healing treatment *in an occult context* will cure, whereas in a nonoccult context, it will have no effect. In other words, if the doctor is either sympathetic with or practices the occult, and he uses the Cayce readings (or American Indian methods, or others), the method may cure the patient. Another doctor, uninterested in the occult but using the same method, will fail. Hence, there is a similarity to psychometry and radionics: it is not the prescription or method that is responsible for the healing but the fact that the one administering it is psychic.

However, we must also note that, regardless of the environment or healer, purely psychological conditions (religious suggestion, psychosomatic remission from placebo factors) and/or treatments relying upon scientifically verifiable methods (e.g., possibly some herbal remedies or unknown, new or forgotten remedies that have healing value in and of themselves) may easily account for a cure rather than direct spiritistic intervention.

WHY THE SPIRITS HEAL

Why should the spirits have an interest in healing, particularly if they are malevolent beings? There are several valid reasons. As Kurt Koch points out, the two commonest threats to man are illness and the uncertainties of the future; hence the occult aims to control those two vital areas. Dr. Koch has demonstrated in many hundreds of cases that most, if not all, occult healings are not true healings. Rather, they represent a shift of the illness from the organic to the psychic (mental-spiritual) and thereby result in illness on a higher level. (See his *Demonology, Past and Present*, chap. 5.)

> In all the cases I have observed over a long period of time, it was only a matter of apparent cure. Either the ailment appeared again after a considerable pause, or there was only a shift, a transfer from the organic to the psychological. . . . a change from bodily ailment to psychological disturbance.[15]

The cost is thus much dearer than any temporary or even total relief from physical suffering. What can be described only as an occult bondage sets in: a predisposition toward the occult and a simultaneous hardening against God and Christ.[16] (As we have noted, most psychics believe in God, but a God of their own making—impersonal or pantheist, never the biblical God.) With spiritual hardening come emotional problems. Those may take longer to appear, but in one way or another the person healed suffers psychically the consequences of occult involvement.

As mentioned earlier, the patient also runs the risk of subjecting his descendants to an ongoing occult curse. Dr. Koch states: "The mass of examples and observations which have been collected through the years paint a shocking picture of the spiritual devastations which result from the activity of occult healers in every branch of this disastrous profession."[17] He cites the case of a young woman in her family's fourth generation of occult practice, who was suffering from severe psychological problems. Her family history revealed that her great-grandfather had hanged himself. Her grandfather had been crushed to death in an accident. His brother had also died in a strange accident. Her father had strangled his wife and then committed suicide. Her father's sister had jumped into the well in front of the house and drowned herself. "One murder, two fatal accidents, three suicides—that is the terrible balance sheet of this family," Koch writes.[18] These examples are by no means uncommon; he cites many similar incidents in his various books.

An important feature of demonology is reciprocation. It is a recurring theme in historic and contemporary occultism. A person may gain occult power or what seems to be a healing, but there is always a price to pay. In primitive societies, that price involves direct worship, subservience, and bondage to the spirits. In 1 Corinthians 10:20, Paul states that those things Gentiles sacrifice, they sacrifice to demons and not to God. In our modern, sophisticated culture the price usually involves indirect worship in the form of adopting an occult world view and a resultant control over the person's life, which insulates one against biblical Christianity. Ultimately, a costly exchange takes place. The seeker is given temporary occult authority and knowledge in return for control over his life and even his soul. Anyone occultly involved who either seeks release or turns to Christ will soon discover how great that control is. Occult users are people in bondage, and deliverance can only come through Christ.

There is another reason demons heal—the activity helps to "primitivize" a culture. For example, in psychic surgery the unsanitary conditions, reliance on spirits, and the anti- or supra-scientific manifestations all have an underlying message. Gary K. North comments:

> These healers have an almost philosophical commitment to unsterile operations. This is not to say that people are actually infected. Indeed, from the

reported cases of infection—virtually none—there is far less infection in one of these primitive clinics than in a typical North American hospital, with its staph infections and other horrors. The bodies of those treated are not infected, but what is infected is the attitude of the public toward standards of cleanliness. The lack of sanitation is a visible testimony against the law of cause and effect in the medical realm. The relationship between cleanliness and health is symbolically rejected by these healers. Those peasants who are treated by them remain in a kind of microbiological bondage to their primitive culture. They remain dependent upon the charismatic healers who alone seem to be able to provide efficacious treatment within the framework of the traditional culture to which these people are clinging. These static cultures are kept static, in part, by the very success of these healers. . . .

Demonic healing is the denial of progress, the denial of widespread public health, the denial of cause and effect, not because it is invariably and necessarily fraudulent, but because it is externally, visibly, miraculously successful in a "statistically significant number of cases." The curse of demonic healing is not that it never really works, except in cases of psychosomatic illness—and all healings that do take place, say orthodox scientists, by definition were psychosomatic in origin—but that it so often relieves the visible symptoms of sickness. The primitive peasants who go to these healers, not being trained in modern universities, have no prior incentive to shut their eyes to the obvious manifestations of healing. They permit themselves to accept what their eyes can see, unlike Western scientists. They are, therefore, willing to place their bodies under the control of the agents of demons and demons themselves. The epistemological protection of autonomous Western science is not present.

Christians must understand the nature of a society like Brazil. It may be able to telescope its progression from primitive religion to Western science and religious skepticism to post-1965 paranormal science and parapsychological fascination. It may be able to skip the rationalist phase. Skeptical rationalism may never get a strong enough foothold, even among the intellectual elite, to secularize the culture. This fact is extremely important, for it has made it very difficult for Christian evangelism by denominations that have a puritan-like commitment to education and rational techniques. Long-term economic growth is made far less likely; mass inflation will be the substitute. The foundations of progress are simply not present, for the primary foundations are matters of faith and attitude.[19]

Primitive societies are hard to evangelize, and psychic healing promotes primitivism. It serves demonic purposes well.

THE QUESTION OF FRAUD

Nearly every book written on psychic surgery contains accounts of fraud perpetrated by both fake and genuine healers. In the former case, a great deal of money can be taken from desperate but well-to-do Westerners. But even genuine healers have no control over their powers, and when they fail they feel the need to "keep up the show." Many of them resort to trickery. The fact that they do so indicates their low regard for human life. Guy L. Playfair states:

You cannot very well pretend to play a piano concerto if you cannot play it.

But the medium can pretend to be a medium, knowing that there is a good chance nobody will notice the difference, since so much of his work deals with the invisible. When he has one of his bad days, he can either cheat on purpose or unconsciously; if he is very honest he will call off the session altogether. If there are two or three hundred people waiting to see him, perhaps people who have a contribution to the centre where he works, he may feel obliged to perform just to satisfy his audience, even if he knows he cannot produce the genuine effects they have come to see.[20]

A healer can always pretend to do an operation on the etheric (invisible) "body," and no one will know the difference, even if there really were one. Playfair discusses this ruse and other, more esoteric shams:

> A far easier way of cheating for beginners is to claim that you are only going to operate on the perispirit body, or in the astral plane. Here, all you have to do is wave your hands in the air above the body, manipulate invisible scissors, knives and other implements, muttering instructions to your unseen helpers. These, of course, will not reply, but everybody present will understand that they are on the astral plane and only you can hear them.
>
> As for diagnosis, you use the time-honored methods of muscle reading and fishing. Chances are your patients have something wrong in the stomach area, so you simply prod around here and write out a prescription for anything you like, preferably something totally harmless. Assure your patients that your spirit guides will slip something into the medicine to make it work better, slap them on the back and order God to be with them. You may find that some will actually get better!
>
> If you come up against a really tough case, you always have karma to fall back on. Supposing an attractive young lady comes up and says:
>
> "Oh, Dr. Wu," (that's your spirit guide) "I'm desperate. I've got cancer of the uterus, colon, stomach, lungs, neck, nose and big toe. I've been given three weeks to live. Help!"
>
> In cases like this you prod her around a little, look

at the ceiling, cock your ear to the voice of your invisible mentor and reply:

"Yes, my dear sister. Your problem is one of karma. In your past incarnation you were a prison guard in Siberia, and before that you were one of the assistants who threw Christians to the lions in Rome. Before that you were a mass murderer in Atlantis, and in the Mesolithic Age you were a child rapist. In this lifetime, you have been given a great chance to pay off all your past debts at once. God is good. Next patient, please."

This will never fail. Karma is karma and Spiritists everywhere love it. Your patient will obediently go away and die, convinced she is doing herself a favor. Your spiritual wisdom and understanding will be widely praised, especially if you murmur a prayer for the girl's soul and wish it better luck next time round.[21]

Playfair notes that even the spirits themselves appeal to the use of karma. Naturally, according to them, all incurable cases result from karmic disorders, and we cannot expect even the spirits to heal fate.

It is also possible that some psychic surgery is not really performed but is suggested to the observer's mind by hypnosis. In other cases, optical illusions are used.

But the majority of the earlier and later observers are agreed that, by a trick of illusion, the *machi* makes the audience believe that she opens the patient's belly and exposes his entrails and liver. According to Father Housse, the *machi* "appears to open the sufferer's body, feels about in it, and extracts something from it." She then exhibits the cause of the illness: a pebble, a worm, an insect. The "wound" is believed to close of itself. But since the usual cure does not involve an apparent opening of the body but merely suction (sometimes to the

point of drawing blood) applied to the part of the
body indicated by the spirit, it is highly probable
that we here have an aberrant application of a
well-known initiatory technique: the neophyte's
body is magically opened to give him a new set of
inner organs and cause his "rebirth."[22]

Other fraudulent methods include the use of hidden capsules filled with blood, hidden animal and
plant tissue, and sleight of hand. Cases of fraud are
so evident and well discussed elsewhere there is no
need to dwell on them here. However, many investigators wrongly conclude that because there are
many cases of trickery, psychic surgery is entirely a
fraud. William Nolen, in *Healing: A Doctor in Search
of a Miracle*, gives the impression that all psychic
surgeons are fakes. However, reading Stanley
Krippner and Alberto Villoldo's critical analysis of
Nolen in *The Realms of Healing*, or the discussions
of psychic surgery in George W. Meeks's *Healers
and the Healing Process*, alters that impression.

Unfortunately psychic healing is real. Just why it
works is the issue.

Extent of the "Cures"

There are two crucial points here. The first is that
the surgery often "cures" the patient *without* alter-
ing his physical condition. Those cures are usually
temporary. The second point is that the material removed (blood, tissue, and so forth) is usually not the
patient's, but stuff apported and materialized from
elsewhere by the spirits. The material is sometimes
found to be animal blood and tissue or vegetable
matter. That is why many investigators believe that
psychic healing is totally fraudulent, and also why
many psychic surgeons are reluctant to let the "diseased tissue" be removed for laboratory analysis.

When it has been tested, it has often proved to be of nonhuman origin. (There are exceptions—sometimes the tumor, blood, or tissue tests out as human. Whether it is *the patient's* is another question.)

It must be noted that these healings are *supernatural*, not physical, and the blood and tissue is produced by the demonic control for "show," for effect, for the patient's benefit. The spirits have apparently told their surgeons that they must produce material to make the patient think, *If I see myself opened up, blood present, and diseased tissue removed, then I must have been healed.* Perhaps that is simply a novel way to use the power of suggestion, and indeed, in many cases the cures of psychic surgery do appear to be only temporary (the suggestion wears off).

Yet there is clearly something else operating here. Valentine reports on a Michigan steel worker, Joe Reffner, who had a miraculous cure:

> "I was scared, but I didn't feel any pain. I saw him cut into me with his bare hands and dig something out. I saw it open, I saw it close, and I saw blood. A guy who said he was a doctor asked me if he could put his hand into my wound. I said it was okay by me if it was clean. He put his hand in, and I could feel it. When he drew it out, it was covered with blood. Then Tony took his hands out, and the wound was instantly healed. He said to me, 'Get up and walk.' I didn't think I could—you know, after surgery and all—but I did. Tony then said, 'Go home and rest,' but some doctors examined me first, and it seemed they couldn't believe what they had seen."

Reffner returned to his hotel—walking without pain and without his crutches for the first time in nearly a decade. His spirits soared. . . .

Reffner's problems were magnified when, later, X-rays revealed that his bones were still broken. He should not have been able to walk, despite the obvious fact that he was walking and picking people up to prove his back was strong. Agpaoa had not mended his bones, but he had removed the pain.[23]

This case suggests the possibility of some hypnotic influence over Reffner and others like him, which by-passes normal brain activity. If so, the hypnosis is exceptionally long-lasting and is performed without the patient's or observer's ability to detect it. But the fact that such a patient can perform normally without either a physical change or further injury during subsequent activity, suggests something more than hypnosis alone. If we suggest a placebo effect, the point at which the effects of mental power alone end and the demonic begin is obviously difficult to determine.

The fact that many times people are not physically changed and yet are "cured" and can function as if they did not still have the ailment is most perplexing. Valentine cites several other cases, including that of a crippled woman who had a broken hip bone braced with a large metal pin, a plate, and five screws. She was operated on by Agpaoa, and after the hip "surgery" he held up a piece of metal and some screws, declaring he had removed four of the screws and the metal plate and that his patient was cured. The lady was able to walk without pain, and even dance, for over a year. Finally, skeptical friends asked her to have an X-ray to prove the plate and screws had really been removed. They were still in place.[24]

Is the power of the mind really that strong? We are convinced that some other factor is operating, at least in some of those nonorganic cures.

The parapsychologists, in keeping with their occult orientation, have put forth the idea that the astral body is the key. Psychic physician-homeopath Sigrun Seutemann states:

The etheric body influences all functions of, and controls the metabolism of, the physical body. . . . It is my conviction that most of the work done by the healer is at the level of the etheric body. Only after this body is restored to normal balance can the healing result in the organs of the *physical* body. . . . The scientists and other researchers observing Tony [Agpaoa] during an "operation" have often been heard to observe, "Tony seems to be in trance only from his shoulders down. He appears to be entirely unconscious of the movement being made by his hands." His invisible work appears to me as being of far more importance to the healing than anything which is visible. The criterion for successful healing is not the effect on the physical body but the changes brought about at the patient's etheric level of existence.[25]

Of course, no evidence whatever exists to support the notion of an "etheric body," let alone the idea that it would have any relation to the physical body even if it did exist. However, it is important to understand what psychic healers are saying here—that medical help is of little or no value unless one is first operated on by psychic healers, who, unlike physicians, can "heal" the astral body. In other words, if one desires healing, one must turn to the occult and forget the medical, since true healing, it is claimed, begins with the etheric, or nonphysical.

Such are the fruits of allowing occult teaching to gain respectability. Such teaching can never be proved, but it can have tremendous impact on those who believe it. Here also lies one of the dangers of parapsychology: "scientific" respectability is given to ideas, concepts, and world views that lead people into occult bondage. In true science, such ideas are never considered.

If we examine the literature of psychic healing we find that psychic diagnosticians and surgeons write prescriptions for obsolete or abnormally high, even lethal, amounts of medicine—sometimes even for poison—and the patient is helped or instantly cured. In one case, enough "medicine" was prescribed to kill a dozen people. Such prescriptions seem to work only for the healer and his patients. They are either ineffective or harmful when used by others. Apparently, if this is not psychosomatic, we have a radionics type of effect here. The medicine is not the crucial factor—the healer and his spirits are. There appears to be both physical and nonphysical work done on the patient by the demons.[26]

It seems that just as the mind can be influenced and even totally controlled by spirits, so can the physiological-anatomical functioning of the body. That would not involve direct possession but rather selective control over, or interruption of, normal mental and physical functions. Perhaps that explains why some people can, for example, walk with broken bones or endure abnormally large doses of medicine.

It may also be true that, after the surgery, if the patient does not take his medicine he may become sick until he does, again furthering his reliance upon occult methods.

CURE RATES

In discussing demonic healing, it should be made clear that despite claims to the contrary, the actual number of true supernatural healings may be comparatively small, although the number of suggestive or psychosomatic healings is significantly larger. In each case, the impact on the person will be the same; the fostering of trust in occult supernaturalism. Since the majority of illnesses (50-80 percent) are psychosomatic, placebo effects alone will always cure a large number of patients. A great many claims to healing are, in fact, produced more by the psychological atmosphere in which the healing takes place than the healing methods themselves or anything supernatural. If a disease is produced by the mind (e.g., an ulcer), and the mind can be convinced the disease is either healed or on the way toward healing, it may well be. This is not to say, however, that true demonic healing never takes place.

Studies (some of higher quality than others) have been conducted on the effectiveness of psychic healing. Several extensive studies done at Lourdes by Bertrin, Benson, Rouby, and others indicate that the true healings are miniscule—estimates vary at between .0004 and 1 percent. Of a probable ten million pilgrims up to the year 1908, the fiftieth anniversary of the vision, possibly 3,962 registered cures (partial or full) were reported, or .0004 percent.[27] Of course, we have no idea how many *unreported* cures there have been. *Whether or not* there is an actual cure, of equal interest is the philosophy held to and promulgated by the *hope* of a cure.

In using more objective criteria for healing (as opposed to self-reports), O. J. West found only 11 cases at Lourdes between 1946 and 1956 that came close to actually being cured.[28] Some objective criteria that have been suggested are:

1. Certification of the patient's condition before and after the visit
2. The finding of organic or incurable illness
3. Immediate recovery and disappearance of the existing pathology
4. Persistence of cure after the visit[29]

Dr. Louis Rose, after twenty years of studying the claims of faith healers, particularly of medium Harry Edwards (who claimed an 80-90 percent healing rate), also found meager confirmation of cures. In a detailed study of 100 of Edwards's "cures," he found 58 cases with incomplete records and unconfirmed claims; 22 cases with records "so much at variance with the claims that it was considered impossible to continue with the investigation further"; two cases of possible cure; one case of definite relief or cure; three cases that improved but later relapsed; four cases of significant improvement; five cases of improvement that were concurrently receiving orthodox medical treatment; and one case of continued deterioration.[30] Edwards's own book, *The Evidence for Spirit Healing* (1953), contains over 10,000 pieces of written testimony from patients claiming to have been helped. Rose's sample was only 1 percent of that monumental collection, but it is obvious that many claims to healing are both inadequately investigated and exaggerated. Strauch's study of 650 patients of Kurt Trampler indicated that after up to fourteen months, 61 percent felt improved, but only 11 percent had objectively measured improvements.[31] A preliminary and admittedly incomplete analysis of 1200 patients having psychic surgery indicated:

 2% healed instantly
10% partially healed at the end of a 10 to 14 day stay in the Philippines
30% partially healed within one month
30% "felt better and some medical tests confirmed improvement in three to six months"
18% were patients which could not be followed up
10% remained unaffected[32]

In other words, 70 percent felt somewhat better, with varying degrees of medical confirmation. However, how long those patients remained improved is unknown.

The problems in determining the effectiveness of

psychic healing are legion, so the above statistics are tentative. Researcher bias, subjective accounts, inadequate data, poor sampling and controls—all play their part. Very few healers, if any, keep adequate records, and it is next to impossible to determine the exact percentage of those truly healed. All we can say is that it appears, at least by the objective measures cited, that the number of patients healed by psychic means is much lower than many healers would have us believe. At the same time, because of various problems in research, there are probably more true psychic healings than the scientific statistics or the critical researcher would have us believe. Statistical methods are rarely used by psychic healers (even in the US, not to mention primitive cultures), and skeptical researchers often are not allowed to witness healings (lest they negatively affect the outcome or the healer's power).

Krippner and Villoldo cite another factor that gives rise to at least a fair number of claims of success among healers:

> Furthermore, those observers who fail to see any evidence of psi in "psychic healing" generally agree that something happens to a healee at least some of the time. In *Healing: A Doctor in Search of a Miracle*, William A. Nolen has concluded that he could not find a single case of a "miraculous" cure. Nevertheless, he admitted that
>
> . . . .half the patients who go to the office of a general practitioner have diseases or complaints that are self-limited, e.g., the common cold. No matter what anyone does for these people, they are going to get better. So the healers are going to achieve at least a 50 per cent cure rate, even if they do nothing. Add to that 50 per cent those patients whom the healers cure of functional disabilities—tension headaches, for example—and they are going to achieve an overall cure rate

> of 70 per cent. We may as well admit this: it's a fact. ["When medicine and mediums get together, humanity will get 70% better," says psychic surgeon Edivaldo.][33]
>
> In other words, we need theories to explain how "healing" happens even if it eventually turns out that psi plays a limited role—or no part at all—in the process. These theories should be open-ended enough so that they can be adapted to "psychic healing" phenomena if they ever reach the level of repeatable observations.[34]

Of course, determining just *how* the healing occurs will demand a much greater effort in studying the methods and results of occult practices. That research in turn can only lead to further occult bondage for the individuals involved and, in the end, for their cultures.

Another difficulty in substantiating psychic healing "cures" is that they are often temporary, as the following example reported by Dr. Naegeli-Osjord illustrates:

> Two of my schizophrenic patients, by their own wish, were treated by Tony Agpaoa. One was "operated" upon in "bloody fashion" in my presence. It appeared as though strands of nerves were being cut out of the brain and removed, but it may be presumed that this was materialization. Cinematography of the process was permitted but I was not allowed to preserve the removed strands to have them examined. Both patients appeared to be very relaxed and normal immediately after the treatment and also on the following days. However, after 3 to 4 months, a relapse occurred, and today, after two years, the situation is unchanged.[35]

He also points out that those who undergo several treatments by the surgeon have a greater chance of being healed than if only one treatment or operation is performed. It would stand to reason that the patient's occult allegiance would increase correspondingly.

In a number of cases, psychic healing and surgery have actually made the patient worse.[36] Many of the sick return bitter and disillusioned, with nothing to show but the loss of thousands of dollars and critical time.

- George Allen had 8 unsuccessful operations by Agpaoa.
- Wilbur Shadley underwent a "successful" operation for lung cancer. The disease was diagnosed as an imbalance of *ying and yang* in the body. After having it "put in balance," he died a month later.
- Young Joey Sutika remains paralyzed after a fake operation.
- Stanley Babiuk was treated in the wrong part of the body for an ailment he never had.[37]

Even in the genuine cases of healing there is the serious cost factor of what Kurt Koch refers to as "the terrible oppression" that visits those who have such operations. "The organic healing is compensated for by the most severe psychical complications." He tells of one healed patient who subsequently underwent psychotherapy for months in an attempt to gain psychological relief but reportedly did not receive even the slightest help.[38]

That brings us to an important point. Emotional problems stemming from occult involvement are remedied not through psychotherapy but through repentance and deliverance through Christ, making use of Christian-oriented psychotherapy. Secular counseling is powerless against the effects of demonism, due both to denying its very existence and to treating the symptoms rather than the cause.

It is significant that psychic healers are rarely able

to heal *themselves*. Playfair states that "Maria" is like all other healers in that "she seems unable to cure her own ailments; it appears to be a rule that spirit doctors pay little attention to their mediums' needs."[39] Dr. Andrija (Henry) Puharich, who spent years analyzing Arigo, says that he "never saw Arigo heal himself, and to my knowledge, in the twenty years in which he practiced, he was never able to heal any organic illness in any blood relative. This is a curious aspect of healing which is difficult to rationalize."[40]

The vast majority of occult healings, like natural healings, are gradual and occur over a period of many weeks or months. Often they require numerous treatments of "surgery," "magnetic passes," or "energy alignment." We might contrast that with the healings of Christ and the apostles, the latter very common men, who healed instantaneously and completely. (At least one of the two exceptions was to teach a spiritual lesson and was obviously no reflection on Jesus' power. The blind man of John 9:6 needed to demonstrate his faith by "going and washing." Mark 8:24 is more difficult, but in any case, both healings were total and nearly instantaneous.)

THE FAITH FACTOR

There is a relationship between occult healing and faith. Satan mimics God even in this area (Hebrews 11:6). In the ten-years' research described in *Healers and the Healing Process* that relationship comes out time and again:

- "Agpaoa can treat 100 Filipinos a day with ease [patients are sympathetic to the occult-animist world view], yet only 50 Europeans require much greater effort."[41]

- Supernatural tooth pulling is common among some surgeons [the mesmerists did it as well].[42] They can simply lift a tooth out of the gum, exerting no effort, even though it is tightly held in its socket. Although the surgeon can do this easily with the native spiritist population or *the believing parapsychologist*, "the same healer may fail in pulling the already loose tooth of a Western foreigner, especially if the patient is a skeptic."[43]

- Similarly, the prescriptions of Arigo work only for his patients. They are useless or dangerous when prescribed by orthodox doctors.

- Psychic healing is more effective if the healer establishes rapport with his patient by producing (occult) spiritual counsel.[44]

- The presence of doubters hinders the psychic's ability. That includes, apparently, all psychic powers, not just healing. Psychometrist Ossoviecki states: "The lucid [psychic] state sometimes arises in a few minutes, and sometimes it takes hours of waiting. This largely depends on the surroundings; skepticism, incredulity (unbelief), or even attention too much concentrated on my person, paralyzes quick success in reading or sensation."[45] The presence of praying Christians stops it entirely.[46]

- Successful investigation of psychic healing demands a sympathetic and open attitude on the part of the investigator. In a sense, they must open themselves up to becoming mediumistically inclined. (Occultists who teach parapsychologists on psychic matters may easily transfer their powers to them.)[47] As Meek states, the last seventy-five years of psychical research have proved that a certain "safe" environment is vital to the production of mediumistic phenomena. It "is impractical to move a mediumistic Filipino healer into a well-equipped scientific laboratory and expect useful results in such surroundings, particularly if the research staff is composed at least in part, of skeptics."[48]

On the contrary, "the healer himself must become totally convinced that the investigators are sympathetic to the cause of paranormal healing and that the researchers have enough knowledge of mediumship and of the medium's connections with other states of consciousness and planes of being to be sympathetic to the idea that the phenomenon cannot always be produced 'on demand.' This same empathy must be established with each individual on the research team. Parapsychology research in the U.S.S.R. has clearly established just how critical this factor is in the production of the paranormal."[49]

- We have mentioned that the blood, tissue, and so forth, are apported, materialized items for the purpose of producing a certain effect. *They are present only to induce faith in the one being healed*, and his faith in the healers, the operation and the occult. (That is true of shamanism as well.)[50]

The healer sometimes will make positive diagnosis in a very confident manner either by a spiritual "x-ray" or by automatic writing. In the latter technique an entity on a higher plane presumably assists the healer in making an accurate diagnosis. At any rate, subconsciously the patient is assured that he or she has finally found someone who truly understands the problem—and has a solution.

The "operation" is usually performed in the presence of others who will be "operated" on the same day. They witness what appear to be tumors, blood clots and various forms of witchcraft items being painlessly extracted from a patient's body in the dramatic setting of a bloody operative field.

This very impressive display assures the prospective patient that something truly miraculous is happening. The subconscious impact of one seeing the alleged tumor that has been plaguing him for so many years being removed from his body and discarded before his very eyes has a profound psychological effect, which undoubtedly can bring about physiological, metabolic, possibly even physical changes. I speculate that on the physical level these changes are probably mediated through the hypothalamus and the autonomic nervous system.

The combination of the motivation, fear, expectation, commitment and the visual effect of "psychic surgery" no doubt are sufficient to initiate an attitudinal change at a level sufficiently deep to bring about a remission or cure in many of the patients who have journeyed to the Philippines in serious hope of improving their health."[51]

- Finally, it should be noted that the faith factor is so strong that, in primitive culture, even Western medicine in some cases does not work as it should.[52]

Belief is very important, even in cures beyond the psychosomatic. In normal consciousness there is a God-given barrier against the demonic, and a healthy distrust of the demonic at least inhibits its effectiveness. There is also more than simply faith or doubt operating here. It is a matter of personal *will*—choice. Deliberate faith in demons gives them the go-ahead to perform miracles. A deliberate aversion to opening oneself to them stops or at least hinders them. That is true culturally as well as individually. Hence we must be very careful about what we choose to believe. If it was true that even Jesus Christ on occasion did not perform "many miracles

. . . because of their unbelief" (Matthew 13:58), it must be true of the negative spirit world as well.

However, skeptics can be psychically healed if they open themselves to the possibility of the event. Lawrence LeShan states that in some of his healing, curiously, results are as good with skeptics as with believers.[53] That is probably due to the extent of his altered state of consciousness and the openness of the healee. Healing appears to depend on the *degree* of either trust or rejection. The unwillingness of a person to open his will to demons is crucial in stopping their activity. And although faith can be present even in doubt, it cannot be present in unbelief. Unfortunately, it is precisely those who never go to healers who are the protected ones. One's very presence in a healing session indicates *some* hope, *some* faith.

EFFECT OF SPIRIT HEALING ON A POPULATION

Psychic healing supports an occult outlook on the world that helps foster dependence on nonbiblical supernaturalism and, ultimately, demonic control over men, as can be seen in some primitive, animistic, or occultly dominated cultures. Tom Valentine mentions a case where Agpaoa was told by his spirit to treat an incurable and fatal bone marrow disease of the head and shoulders by operating on the chest. The patient reported, "I felt fantastic while I was lying there; something vibrant pervaded my being. Tony removed what looked like a tremendous mass of cartilage and blood." Five years late the woman still had no sign of the disease. Valentine comments: "Taking the disease out of her chest rather than where doctors knew it existed hints broadly that this phenomenon defies physical laws in every sense."[54]

It does more than just defy physical laws—it fosters distrust in them, and even in the concept of common sense. Dr. North commented perceptively on this when discussing the case of a girl who had tropical leaves removed from her stomach:

> How can we explain this? Fakery? At eighteen inches, in front of cameras and many witnesses? Yet how could leaves get into a woman's intestinal area? Aborigines in Australia believe that when a hex using a "death bone" is made, a second bone literally enters the victim and kills him, either directly or by the sorcerer's burying the death bone, burning it, or in some way destroying it. Can this be correct? Is this analogous to the Filipino housemaid's rash, which was treated by pulling rice-sized pellets through microscopically small pores? What has a leaf in common with pellets?
>
> There is no logical answer simply because such phenomena are not governed by rational categories. What is more likely than the idea that such items do reside inside men's systems is to assume some form of demonic transformation. The pellets and the leaves are literally materialized, either by the healer's control agent, or by some other occult source of power. In other words, the victim of witchcraft is under spiritual bondage, and this bondage has physical aspects, such as a feeling of illness or discomfort.
>
> But these feelings are not those that would be caused if real leaves were inside the body. No Western physician could operate on the victim and discover leaves inside the body, or pellets instead of a rash. The visible signs that are produced when the spirit control agent of the healer works on the bodies of the victims are a means of confirmation to primitive people that the occult is directly involved. The leaves become tangible symbols of demonic power, confusing to the Western observer, but understood in principle by the local population. The local tribes-

man nods in agreement with the healer's diagnosis: yes, it must have been witchcraft.

The sight of the abnormal affirms the existence of occult power, thereby increasing men's fear of the local medicine man or village sorcerer who must have produced the hex. Seeing, after all, is believing—unless you are a Western observer. For the Westerner, seeing is also believing, but the belief is in sleight of hand by men, not a kind of sleight of hand by demons. But the effect on the tribe is the same, whoever is playing games: continued occult bondage and perpetual fear in a world of unfamiliar laws and hostile forces—intensely personal forces.[55]

Dr. North's conclusion is worth pondering:

Western rationalism is as one-sided and narrow as any other world-and-life view. Those who hold to its premises have exercised great power over the last two centuries. Much of this power is well deserved. By refining the techniques of science, Western think- ers have made possible a flowering of human cul- ture that is the envy of the primitive, magical world. The whole underdeveloped world wants a piece of our action, but it does not usually want to give up the other aspects of its culture that guarantee continued poverty.

By turning its leaders into socialists, materialists, bureaucrats, and rationalists through scholarships to our better universities, we have cut off the leaders from their popular support. Democracy cannot flourish in these nations for many reasons, not the least of which is the undemocratic nature of all bu- reaucratic rule; and it is bureaucracy, far more than democracy, that has been the West's major organi- zational export—bureaucracy financed by government-to-government foreign aid and heavy taxation inside the recipient nations.

But democracy also cannot flourish where de- monism is present. The essence of demonism is an elitist manipulation of the common tribesmen. The means of power are personal asceticism, demon possession, trances, visions, dreams, and total immersion into the occult. Ritual, not a study of the regularities of nature, is the law of primitive cultures. The ideology of bureaucracy may be in conformity with some of the aspects of demonism, but democracy is in total opposition. No one but a Western intellectual could have believed that India was democratic, or that its traditions and institutions might permit the limited democracy of the liberal West. Indira Gandhi did not cut down Indian democracy at the roots; there never were any roots, except in the dreams and visions of Western commentators and Indian newspaper editorials. And what is true of India is true of the so-called Third World. Where demonism is a part of the culture, democracy cannot take root. Neither can the rationalistic production methods of free-market capitalism.

What is so disturbing today is the growing popularity of the Eastern cosmologies within Western circles, especially among the formally educated young. It is not possible to import Western versions of Eastern philosophy—all nicely sterilized by the professors of Eastern religion on the campuses—without simultaneously opening up one's mind and soul to all the rest of Eastern culture: monism, mysticism, asceticism, irrationalism, and finally magic. The East is coming West. It represents the importation of intellectual and cultural stagnation at best; at worst, it will destroy the very foundations of Western productivity. It is integration into the void.

Everyone wants to "do good." Healing seems to do good. Occult healing seems to do good much more cheaply. Henry Belk, the rich psychic investigator who helped to popularize both Arigo and the Philippine healers, and who is rich because his staunchly Presbyterian father established a cost-effective, economically rational chain of stores, has in classic words described the "benefits" of healing by spirits: "They don't eat, they don't pay taxes, and they supply the labor." At the heart of all magic is the quest for power but at low cost. Asceticism is personal, not cultural. Economically, it is the philosophy of something for nothing. Westerners who think they can make use of Eastern and primitive healing techniques without the personal ascetism required of the healing adepts will find that the price of their power is far, far higher than they think.

Westerners who do accept the validity of the stories concerning psychic healing may say to themselves: "What a shame that we in the West have closed off ourselves to such wonderful powers." Wonderful indeed: filled with wonder. But the same person who is saddened by the absence of occult healing techniques in the West lives in a clean environment and has at his disposal skilled medical diagnosticians operating in terms of the division of labor (meaning physicians can check each other's progress and learn). The Western citizens want the blessings of both cultures, not realizing that what primitive man has is a curse.

Now we find men who are out to fuse Western technology and Eastern irrationalism. They are out to build an electric Tibet. They fail to comprehend that in an electric Tibet, not even the machines would be healthy. A Tibetan culture does not accent a Western view of the world in which man can gain access to electrical power, thereby increasing the productivity of all people, not just the demonic elite. We cannot fuse the two cultures; the two cultures are at war.[56]

THE PHILOSOPHY OF OCCULT HEALERS

One factor clearly betraying spiritual healing as occultic is the fact that healers may simultaneously engage in fortune-telling and a wide variety of other occult powers along with healing. Their philosophy is consistently antibiblical. Even though their world view is almost universally religious, and many claim to be Christians, their philosophy is inevitably reincarnationist, pantheist, animist, monist, or syncretist. The fact that most healers view their powers as a gift from God again points to the fact that natural man supposes true healing is beyond the natural human capacity.

If we examine the beliefs of the healers, the kind of religion we are dealing with soon becomes evident. Healer Gorden Turner says, "You see, I don't believe, I can't believe in a personal God."[57] Olga Worrall says, in characteristic pantheism, "God is all."[58] Psychic surgeon Edivaldo openly displays his confused loyalties by stating, "If the devil can relieve pain, open up a stomach and remove an ulcer, then I prefer the devil. . . . Don't give me one [a Bible] because I won't read it. . . . I want to believe in Christ in my own way."[59] Harry Edwards is similarly heretic when he tells us that his spiritual healing has nothing to do with "the Christian theory of vicarious atonement, under which Jesus was supposed to take all the sins of mankind on his shoulders."[60] Dr. Christopher Woodward offers us the enlightening view that we need a new Christ. He says, "We talk in terms of the Universal Christ. Our Christ bears very little resemblance to the traditional *churchianity* Christ, which is about as backward as you could imagine! I mean, the traditional Christian church is the most restricting of the major religions. It's utterly prejudiced by dogma, theology, ritual, all sorts of nonsense, you see."[61] Mr. A. says that his "instructions are that the church is within. . . . from what I get from the Powers, I'm told heaven and hell are right here where we're living."[62] Finally, Rolling Thunder states with conviction: "The earth is a living organism . . . the Great Spirit is the life that is in all things—all the creatures and plants and even the rocks and minerals. All things, and I mean *all* things—have their own will. . . . We all must realize that we all have many lifetimes."[63]

In discussing how his powers begin to operate, one of the most famous psychometrists points out both the necessity of a certain world view and an altered state of consciousness (most all psychics require a similar "attunement"):

> I begin by stopping all reasoning, and I throw all my inner power into perception of spiritual sensation. I affirm that this condition is brought about by my unshakable faith in the spiritual unity of all humanity. I then find myself in a new and special state in which I see and hear outside time and space. . . . Whether I am reading a sealed letter, or finding a lost object, or psychometrising, the sensations are nearly the same.
>
> I seem to lose some energy; my temperature becomes febrile, and the heart beats unequal. . . . As soon as I cease from reasoning, something like electricity flows through my extremities for a few seconds.[64]

Healer Le Shan requires a similar spiritual commitment during the healing process:

> I would then find myself a comfortable standing position (for no particular reason except that I concentrate more easily standing), close my eyes, and conceptualize this particular healee being in both realities at the same time. I would attempt to reach a point of being in which I would know that he not only existed as a separate individual inside his skin and limited by it, but that he also—and in an equally "true" and "real" manner—existed to the furthest reaches of the cosmos in space and time. When I knew for a moment that this was true and that I also coexisted with him in this manner—when, in fact, I had attained the Clairvoyant Reality—the healing work was done.[65]

What we read in the quotations above rings of religion. The "unshakable faith in the spiritual unity of all humanity" and the attainment of "Clairvoyant Reality" speak of spiritual conditions, though not biblical ones.

The religion seemingly manifested is nothing more than an intense degree of what is called humanism, the elevation of common man into the sphere and prerogatives of God. The healers themselves become gods, or at least the favorite contacts of some powerful gods; and they then can master creation, breaking the normal rules and laws and dispensing benevolent favors. As in common religious humanism, man is both god and a part of the creator-god, and given enough power via occult knowledge he can accomplish anything. The religious fervor expressed in the quotations above has in it a kind of arrogance typical not of worship of the true God but rather of His adversary. It is a satanic doctrine that worships the creature rather than the Creator (Romans 1).

Satan's initial attack against mankind was his tempting Eve with the promise of knowledge. She would be "like God," the serpent promised, and would enjoy an enviable state of physical health ("ye shall not surely die"). Adam and Eve ate of the tree of knowledge at the bidding of God's enemy and achieved not immortality but shame and ultimately death. Occultism likewise promises special knowledge and, in its extreme forms, a kind of immortality through a transcendance to a higher plane denied the rest of mankind. Healing is only the beginning; those believing in the religious doctrines of the occult aspire to nothing less than becoming gods themselves.

Notes

1. Jeffrey Mishlove, *The Roots of Consciousness*, p. 151. Copyright 1975 by Random House, Inc. Used by permission.
2. George W. Meek, "The Healers," in George W. Meek, ed., *Healers and the Healing Process*, p. 32. Copyright 1977 by Theosophical Publishing House. Used by permission.
3. Hans Naegeli-Osjord, "Psychiatric and Psychological Considerations," in Meek, p. 86.
4. Sally Hammond, *We Are All Healers*, p. 42.
5. Sally Hammond, "What the Healers Say: A Survey of Healers in Britain," p. 14.
6. Ruth Montgomery, *Born to Heal*, p. 223.
7. Kurt Koch, *Occult Bondage and Deliverance*, p. 42.
8. Amy Wallace and Bill Henkin, *The Psychic Healing Book*, p. 15.
9. Hans Holzer, *Beyond Medicine*, p. 161.
10. Stanley Krippner and Alberto Villoldo, *The Realms of Healing*, p. 95.
11. Ibid.
12. Alfred Stelter, "Psychoenergetic Phenomena," in Meek, p. 77.
13. Tom Valentine, *Psychic Surgery*, p. 51. Copyright 1973. Reprinted with the permission of Contemporary Books, Inc., Chicago.
14. Ronald Rose, *Primitive Psychic Power*, p. 128; Mishlove, pp. 6-7.
15. Kurt Koch, *Christian Counseling and Occultism*, p. 139.
16. See Kurt Koch, *Demonology Past and Present*, p. 121; Koch, *Occult Bondage and Deliverance*, p. 47.
17. Koch, *Christian Counseling and Occultism*, p. 79.
18. Ibid., pp. 134-35, case 66.

19. Gary K. North, *None Dare Call It Witchcraft*, pp. 158, 153-54.
20. Guy L. Playfair, *The Unknown Power*, p. 113. Copyright 1975 by Simon & Schuster. Used by permission.
21. Ibid., pp. 114-15, 169-70.
22. Mircea Eliade, *Shamanism: Archaic Techniques of Ecstasy*, p. 330. Copyright 1972. Reprinted by permission of Princeton University Press.
23. Valentine, pp. 39-40.
24. Ibid., pp. 25-27.
25. Sigrun Seutemann, "A Psychic Physician's Experience," in Meek, pp. 92-93.
26. Playfair, pp. 123-26, 132.
27. Benjamin B. Warfield, *Counterfeit Miracles*, pp. 107, 280.
28. O. J. West, *Eleven Lourdes Miracles*.
29. Jan Ehrenwalk, "Parapsychology and the Healing Arts," in Benjamin B. Wolman, et al, eds., *Handbook of Parapsychology*, p. 546.
30. Ibid., p. 551.
31. Ibid., pp. 551-52.
32. Seutemann, in Meek, p. 93.
33. Playfair, p. 170.
34. Krippner and Villoldo, pp. 252-53.
35. Naegeli-Osjord in Meek, p. 87.
36. William A. Nolen, *Healing: A Doctor in Search of a Miracle*, chapter 4.
37. Valentine, pp. 48-52, photographs.
38. Koch, *Occult Bondage*, p. 43.
39. Playfair, p. 150.
40. Andrija Puharich, "Paranormal Healing in Brazil—Arigo," in Meek, p. 43.
41. Ibid., p. 68.
42. Slater Brown, *The Heyday of Spiritualism*, p. 23.
43. Stelter, in Meek, p. 71.
44. Ibid., pp. 66, 71.

45. Nandor Fodor, *Encyclopaedia of Psychic Science*, p. 319. Copyright 1974 by Citadel Press. Used by permission.
46. See for example Koch, *Occult Bondage*, p. 40.
47. Ibid.
48. George W. Meek and David Hoy, "Deception and Sleight of Hand," in Meek, p. 111.
49. Ibid., pp. 102-3.
50. Michael Harner, ed., *Hallucinogens and Shaminism*, pp. 23-24.
51. Forrest J. Cioppa, "Medical Effectiveness," in Meek, p. 119.
52. Leonard Nimoy, "In Search of Witchdoctors."
53. Lawrence LeShan, *The Medium, the Mystic, and the Physicist*, pp. 117-18.
54. Valentine, pp. 60-61.
55. North, pp. 166-67.
56. Ibid., pp. 168-70.
57. Hammond, *We Are All Healers*, p. 149.
58. Ambrose A. Worrall, and Olga N. Worrall, *Explore Your Psychic World*, p. 1; *Psychic*, April 1972.
59. Playfair, p. 166.
60. Paul Miller, *Born to Heal—A Biography of Harry Edwards*, cited in Koch, *Occult Bondage*, p. 45.
61. Hammond, *We Are All Healers*, p. 183.
62. Montgomery, p. 218.
63. Doug Boyd, *Rolling Thunder*, p. 52; Krippner and Villoldo, p. 69.
64. Fodor, p. 319.
65. LeShan, p. 117.

8

The Christian View of Psychic Healing

Unfortunately, those who should be most aware of the dangers of psychic healing are often incredibly naive. Many spiritual and psychological problems are not viewed as having their origin in occult involvement. Parapsychologists encourage this naiveté by discounting the dangers. For example, Hans Holzer, who teaches parapsychology at the New York Institute of Technology, says, "For the record, no psychic healer ever caused anyone any physical harm; the application of unorthodox healing has never worsened any illness."[1] In addition to being false, such a claim implies that psychic healing deals with the physical, when in fact, its most important effects are often spiritual and psychological.

DANGERS TO THE PATIENT

We are very concerned about the negligence of those professionals who believe occultism is safe. Neurosurgeon C. Norman Shealy in his *Occult Medicine Can Save Your Life* advocates many types of occultism, claiming at least potential benefit. He states, "My test for the use of the occult is, can it harm?"[2] He and many like him demonstrate an inexcusable ignorance of the wealth of documentation showing the consequences of occultism. Referring to the hazards of occultism, Dr. Koch states, "I could quote examples of this in detail, yet parapsychologists are unwilling to admit the truth of these things, for if they did so they would be unable to pursue their experiments into clairvoyance and spiritistic mediumship with a clear conscience."

Dr. Koch states further:

> Yet in my forty years of Christian work, and as a result of having counseled something in the region of 20,000 individual people, I have personally come across thousands of cases in which it was the contact with occultism that was the root cause of the problem, and the oppression that was the direct result of this contact. In the light of this, I have often wondered why the scientific research workers of today have been unable to produce any form of argument or proof in support of their dogmatic and a priori assumptions. . . .
>
> If we were to consider the number of cases in which occultism has had a damaging effect on people, our ratio would work out to something in the region of nine out of ten cases. I could support this fact by means of many thousands of examples. Yet scientists persist in saying, "The problem does not exist." If one's counseling work were dependent upon narrow-mindedness like this, one would be driven to despair.[3]

Koch notes that contact with powers alien to God involves a person in idolatry. Occult involvement simply abandons God and serves the devil, which carries only the severest consequences:

> First of all, what is the basic cause of occult subjection? Every sin connected with sorcery cuts a person off from God and turns him towards the worship of idols. And if a person begins to serve the devil, he

will receive the devil's wages. Thus, when a person abandons God, he abandons himself at the same time. There are innumerable passages in the Bible declaring quite clearly that sorcery and occultism are terrible sins which are an abomination to the Lord and a forsaking of the living God. The following are but a few of these passages:

Exodus	7:11-12	1 Samuel	28
Exodus	22:18	1 Chronicles	10:13-14
Leviticus	19:26,31	Isaiah	2:6, 8:19
Leviticus	20:6, 27	Jeremiah	27:9-10
Zechariah	10:2	Galatians	5:20
Malachi	3:5	2 Timothy	3:8
Acts	8:9	Revelation	21:8
Acts	16:16	Revelation	22:15
Acts	19:19		

Anyone who trespasses into Satan's domain by committing sins of sorcery will immediately be harassed by the powers of darkness, irrespective of whether he takes the step consciously or unconsciously. And the effects of this transgression of God's law make themselves felt in . . . different areas of a person's life.[4]

The areas indicated include serious effects in one's spiritual life, character, and mental health, as well as the development of mediumistic abilities. It is interesting that only believers in Christ suffer spiritually—not Hindus, Muslims, Buddhists, or others—except that occult involvement makes it very difficult for a person to become a Christian. Further, "all other religious faiths [except for orthodox Judaism] of the world seem to ally themselves to mediumistic phenomena. Only the Christian faith stands out in sharp contrast to occultism."[5]

Koch states in *Demonology: Past and Present*:

. . . demonic healing always results in an engramm taking place, i.e., a transference from the lower to the upper levels. The original organic illness is

shifted higher into the psychical realm, with the result that while the physical illness disappears, new
disorders appear in the mental and emotional life of
the person concerned, disorders which are in fact
far more difficult to treat and cure. Magical healings
are therefore not really healings at all, but merely
transferences from the organic to the psychical level.

So far so good, but in counseling work one discov-
ers that the problem is even more involved than
what we have just mentioned.

Firstly, one does not realize the force with which
these transfers are accompanied.

Secondly, the transfers cannot be reversed, the
wheel cannot be turned back, except through the
power of Christ.

And thirdly, these magical transfers act as a
blockage to a person's spiritual life.

Because of this, a person who has experienced a
transference of this nature is in need of authoritative
Christian counseling, and experience shows that
only those who are ready and willing to hand their
lives over to Christ completely, can experience deliverance.

The damage caused through magical healing is
immense, and since this damage occurs mainly in
the spiritual lives of the people who are healed, one
is forced to describe the power behind it as demonic. . . .

These demonic healings are only a ruse whereby
Satan, in exchange for organic help, ruins a person's soul.

Demonic healings are not true forms of healing
but merely represent a shift of the problem from the
organic to the psychical realm. The person who is
healed is the victim of a terrible confidence trick.

The effects of these occult forms of healing can
often be seen for years in the spiritual and mental
life of the victim.[6]

Those consequences are not potential; they are
actual. It is not that *some* people are negatively

affected—in light of Koch's writings and our research, we would expect that most if not *all* of those who are occultly healed are likely to suffer either psychologically or spiritually in some way. There are also physical effects. Koch notes, "This is another thing I have often observed; people who are under occult subjection, or even demonized, frequently are in fatal accidents."[7]

Of concern to many physicians is the possibility that the patient's faith in psychic healing could waste enough precious time to prevent cure by orthodox means. A cancer could metastisize, or a lesser ailment could progress to a dangerous stage. There are enough novices and fraudulent healers to make that a concern, particularly when even "legitimate" healers are known to resort to trickery. The problem is especially acute when patients seek psychic surgery. The time involved in a trip to Brazil or the Philippines and the questionable integrity of even the best psychic surgeons, often amount to nothing more than a foolish venture, as many have discovered too late. In psychic surgery, of course, one is totally separated from orthodox medicine and placed in an environment and atmosphere hostile to it. There is the risk of infection, injudiciously applied therapeutic methods, and legions of other concerns (e.g., pressure applied to a detached retina or a fragile spleen).

The actual frequency of true physical healings is so low that the occult consequences are entirely out of proportion to the possible benefits. Even the benefits can carry worse consequences than not being healed. Do we really want to place our physical and spiritual health in the hands of primitive people in trances or new age spiritual healers who depend upon spirit-guides—guides we know nothing about? And if the spirits decide not to heal, can we trust our illnesses to the medically ignorant? Would their advice be reliable? Could a psychic surgeon complicate an already serious problem?

DANGERS TO THE HEALER

The psychic healers themselves, as with mediums, often suffer greatly in their personal lives, although both their spirits' and their own world view assure them that the suffering has nothing to do with contacting forces alien to God. Suffering, it is said, is just a necessary part of spiritual purging and growth. Everyone has his karma to pay.

It is not uncommon for psychic healers, psychic surgeons, and shamans (during healing) to have the patient's sickness temporarily transferred to themselves, causing considerable pain. Koch calls this mediumistic empathy *homeopathic magic*.

Psychic healers, as mediums, derive their healing energy from psychic vampirism of human energy and of the control spirit's own energy. (Even if neutral energy fields exist and are used, it would be difficult if not impossible to distinguish their use from the strategic use of demonic energy.) The spirits do have a great deal of power they can utilize, as even a cursory study of historical or biblical demonology indicates. A serious concern is just what effect that transference of demonic energy *into* a healer might have. It possibly marks the person as "belonging" to the powers of darkness. It may even affect the person at the genetic level, which could account for the apparent hereditary transmission of occult powers and suceptibility as well as for the very powerful mediums that arise after generations of mediumism. Just as certain radiation and chemical imbalance can damage a person's genetics (X-rays, alcohol), so might this energy have negative effects beyond our current understanding.

It is instructive to note that as far as acquisition of powers is concerned, shamans report the same patterns as modern occultists. The powers come through heredity, being chosen by the spirits, or deliberate personal choice.[8] When heredity is claimed, the shaman's powers become evident in childhood, as is true of many modern psychics.

Eliade notes that *nonhereditary* "acquisition of magico-religious [i.e., occult] powers presents an almost infinite number of forms and varients," which is true of modern occultism as well.[9] Eliade also notes the oddity of some cases; for example, one Iglulik shaman became such after being wounded by a walrus. (His mother was also a shaman and had become that by a fireball's entering her.) We find similar examples in Western society. Peter Hurkos, for one, became psychic after hitting his head when he fell off a ladder. But even such strange cases usually involve either hereditary factors or prior occult involvement; the acquisition of psychic powers has nothing to do with the trauma itself, although the spirits may have chosen to use it for purpose of disguise.

When there is no hereditary predisposition, psychic powers are developed very slowly. The spirits conducting the process warn of serious consequences for violation of this rule. It is possible that the transfer of demonic energy resulting in psychic powers slowly alters the central nervous system and conditions it for psychic receptivity.[10]

CLEVER COUNTERFEITS

Kurt Koch points out that numerous Christians have unfortunately labeled healings by either religious suggestion or the demonic as having their origin in God.

Over the years it has become quite obvious to me through my counseling work that all these mediumistic abilities are really a diabolical counterpart to the spiritual gifts bestowed on us by God. The devil is ever trying to imitate God. One can justify this conclusion by the fact that mediumistic forces and powers can always be overcome and halted through the prayers of a believing Christian. Similarly the actual possession of mediumistic abilities is always a hinderance to the development of a sound and healthy Christian life. Therefore, as we have mentioned already, there is nothing worse than when mediumistic powers are ignorantly accepted and labelled as evidences of the workings of the Holy Spirit. And yet this is exactly what is happening among certain extreme Christian groups today.[10]

There is a terrible error being propagated in the world today whereby demonic healings, because of the Christian facade behind which they are placed, are being claimed as charismatic miracles. One minister wrote me a furious letter claiming that his ability to use a pendulum was a gift of God, and as such had to be used for the benefit of mankind. It was unthinkable for him to believe that mediumistic healings are basically occult and not charismatic in character.[11]

Some Christians have a kind of psychic sensitivity and can heal other Christians by essentially mesmeric passes over the body. We believe that the risk here is so high—that so often the power is mediumistic—that such people should not be sought out for help or counsel, particularly if they possessed their powers before becoming believers. Koch notes many cases showing "how dangerous the laying on of hands can be when administered by occultly oppressed Christian workers."[12] That is not to condemn all laying on of hands. It is a biblical practice and is fine when employed by responsible Christian leaders. We only caution against certain questionable cases.

Dr. Koch states that natural magnetism is very weak.

> Strong forms of magnetism are only found in the demonic area. A man who practiced healing magnetism once came to me to be counseled. He told me, "Natural magnetism enables a person to treat only one or two patients each day. Whoever has powers of healing magnetism to treat more than two people a day is plugged in to the underworld."
>
> There are many people, particularly in the Far East, who are able to cure or to help people suffering from headaches, rheumatism, and arthritis by making stroking movements over them with their hands, but whenever I have come across a person who possesses this gift, I have always found that either his parents, grandparents, or great-grandparents have dabbled in magic or spiritism. For this reason, even in the case of natural magnetism I am not altogether happy with its use.[13]

Koch also says:

> Although certain Christian workers believe that some types of healing mesmerism are dependent on neutral rather than mediumistic powers, I would say that I have personally hardly ever come across a neutral form. Many years of experience in this field have shown me that even in the case of Christian mesmerisers the basic mediumship has always come to the surface in the end.[14]

CAN BE TAUGHT

Dr. Koch is convinced that "it is rare today to find someone with a genuine gift of healing."[15] Gifts of healing are usually occultic, although God may use a Christian to heal someone if it is to His purpose. We have not dealt so far with Christian healing. Biblical healing is done through the power of God; it cannot be taught, and it depends ultimately on God's will. He cannot be cajoled to heal, as some "miracle healing services" would have us suppose.

Conversely, psychic healing (or surgery, or diagnosis) *can* be taught if one will apply the appropriate methods of occult disciplines and instruction. Many occult movements and groups today offer classes in spiritual healing; the holistic health movement, Edgar Cayce's A.R.E., the Chaneys' *Astara*, Mormonism,* and spiritism, are some of the major ones. If someone says he can teach you to become a spiritual healer, he is definitely involved in occult healing. God simply does not work in that way.

Historically, occult healing has been associated with specially selected individuals within a culture who had access to the occult mysteries and were the custodians of secret knowledge, which they passed on very carefully and discreetly. Only in our time are we encountering mass efforts to organize classes to teach occult healing. Terte, Philippine psychic surgeon, has taught more than a dozen others to do psychic surgery. He says he "assures each student that if he applies himself he can be certain that he will gradually be attuned to his own spirit protector [guide] and be able to get instructions on both diag-

---

*Mormon theology and practice lead us to define Mormonism as containing occult elements rather than being solely a cult system, for example valid supernatural prophecy that is biblically false, contact with supernatural beings, stress on supernatural gifts. See Bruce McConkie, *Mormon Doctrine* (Salt Lake City, Utah: Bookcraft, 1977), pp. 35-36, 46, 590, 643-51; Bruce McConkie, *Doctrinal New Testament Commentary*, 3 vols. (Salt Lake City, Utah: Bookcraft, 1976) 2:217-18, 232, 240, 277, 320-21, 459; 3:137-41, 225, 393, 553. See also Walter Martin, "The Occultic Side of Mormonism," in *The Maze of Mormonism* (Santa Ana, Calif.: Vision House, 1978), pp. 211-37.

nosis and treatment. . . . He will gradually have help from *more* than one protector."[16] Reflecting his orientation toward *white magic*, his teaching methods include memorization of biblical passages, meditation, and dedication to the cause and philosophy of occultism.

In Britain, the exceptional increase of occult healers (who now number in the thousands) can be traced directly to the efforts of medium Harry Edwards, who developed training courses in spiritual healing. In fact, in every country where occult healing is on the increase, mediums and psychics are teaching courses on healing. This is particularly true of Brazil, with its 40 million followers of spiritism. Each year multitudes of people are occultly healed in Brazil—482,000 in 1975-1976, claims one spiritist center in Sao Paulo.[17] Worldwide, several million people are subjected to occult bondage in the guise of benevolent "healing."

George Meek notes that there is an essential unity in the methods used for teaching healing.[18] He cites healer training programs in the Philippines, Great Britain, Brazil, and the US which, apart from a few expected cultural variables, all utilize the same methods. (Most exceptions were found in the program of Lawrence LeShan, who, as we have stated, prefers to stay away from overt spiritism.) The aspects of the training programs (including LeShan's) in all four countries that were exactly the same were:

1. Encouraging the healer to consider himself a *channel* for healing.
2. Tailoring the course to the student's personal religion and belief system (95 percent of the healers have Eastern-occult metaphysical views, so they are not really flexible; but it should be recognized that most nonbiblical religious systems, including

many liberal Christian systems, have occult or Eastern elements).

3. Teaching (occult) meditation and "attunement" techniques.
4. Encouraging medical doctors to work in conjunction with the healers (The Academy of Parapsychology and Medicine, and the holistic health movement in general are examples of "good name" identification).

Apart from LeShan's, all other healer-training methods in the four countries studied involved:

1. Recommending the use of *magnetic passes*.
2. Specifically encouraging the student to develop clairvoyance and clairaudience.

Finally, and most importantly, all programs "teach the patient to solicit help from spirit entities for both diagnostic and healing purposes."[19]

DEMONIC ACTIVITY

Despite man's optimism concerning discovering "new" innate powers, he simply does not have the equipment—personal or technological—to cope with what are actually demonic manifestations. Dr. North points out that modern man is not only powerless to deal with the supernatural manifestations of demonism, but even unwilling to acknowledge them as such:

> The possession of Arigo by a demon should be clear to anyone who takes seriously the biblical doctrine that it is appointed once for man to die and after this, the judgment. It was not a floating soul of a dead physician. Physicians do not have the power to perform the kind of surgery Arigo performed, not even dead Prussian physicians. The ability of Arigo to halt the flow of blood—an ability demonstrated on

numerous occasions—is not medical; it is supernatural. . . .

Modern science cannot handle the facts of paranormal science. Each of the major researchers will go so far into these studies of the scientifically impossible, convincing himself, step by step, that he is only investigating the statistically improbable. Dr. Thelma Moss calls her book *The Probability of the Impossible*, which she tries to make acceptable by dealing with these scientifically impossible facts in terms of the *as yet unknown*. What Dr. Moss and her professional kinsmen will not face is the fact that there is a demonic realm of life—not just a metaphor of evil, but demonic activity in the realm of Kantian phenomena, that is, the denial of Kant's neat cleavage between the unknown and the scientifically known.

Puharich's account of Uri Geller is so totally improbable that one wonders why, apart from the expectation of enormous profit, any respectability-seeking publisher would have touched it. Messages from intergalactic robot ships, self-destructing cassette tapes, and on and on. Puharich could put his name on *Uri*, yet he feared, back in 1963 anyway, to consider the possibility that spirit possession is a fact of life. Anything might be true, except that. Let spirits of dead men into your universe, and the idea of a God who acts in history gets much too close for comfort. Let demons in, and you cannot protect yourself any longer without allowing God in, too—and that, above all, is what secular man dares not contemplate. . . .

Belk and Puharich, as paranormal researchers, wanted more data. They were still operating under the delusion that if you can just gather enough examples of impossible events, orthodox scientists will accept their reality and reformulate their concepts of what is and is not possible. But all you should expect is that numerous impossible events are only marginally more difficult to dismiss than a single impossible event.

It becomes a matter of rejecting a large sample of events as being either statistically insignificant (which is almost always the case, given the non-repeatability of most occult phenomena) or insignificant because of statistical fluke. The scientists will send the researcher back to tighten his controls and/or increase his sample until signs of the paranormal disappear. Only then will the orthodox scientist accept the verdict of the experiments. The conflict is at bottom religious. The orthodox scientist stands at the edge of a bottomless pit, daring the paranormal scientist to present another fact that cannot be explained by means of orthodox categories. Then he shovels it over his back and calls for more facts.

But Puharich, like all paranormal researchers, cannot grasp this fact. After all, they themselves have found the evidence compelling—up to a point. Not "over the line" into the occult, but compelling to an extent great enough to get them laughed off any orthodox podium. Once they have the facts, they try to explain them. They simply cannot do this, given their commitment to the standards of scientific investigation and correlation. But they try. They reach for explanations like Dr. Jule Eisenbud's psychoanalytic explanation of Ted Serios' mental photography. They press on, undaunted by skepticism, though not unaffected by it. They cease asking questions that are too embarrassing—the absolutely crucial questions, in other words.

When Puharich returned to the United States after his first visit to see Arigo in action, he began a series of experiments that are only too typical of the pathetic attempted fusion of demonic possession and orthodox scientific inquiry—as if the two were not totally antithetical in both theory and practice. He felt compelled to continue true research. Not acknowledging the demonic nature of Arigo's healing abilities, Puharich and Dr. Luis Cortes of the New York University School of Medicine attempted to imitate Arigo's techniques.

First, they took rats as their victims. "Using painstaking care, Cortes held a rat firmly while Puharich tried to insert a small knife under the lid and up toward the sinus cavities. They found that it was literally impossible to do this on a conscious, unanesthetized rat unless its head was held in a viselike grip." Surprise, surprise! Rats simply do not like to have knives stuck into their eyes.

But rats are not people, as even a fairly large percentage of experimental psychologists know. What would people think of having a physician stick knives into their eyes? Fortunately, a subject was eagerly awaiting just such an experiment. A young laboratory assistant, fascinated with the stories she had heard about Arigo, insisted that they try Arigo's trick on her. Neither of them wanted to try this, the author writes, but "she kept on insisting. . . ."

Cortes took a small knife and began to insert it into her eye. It went in only a fraction of an inch under her eyelid, when the girl signaled that she could not stand the pain. "The experience convinced all three that they were dealing with an extraordinary case in Arigo that would be a mammoth challenge to science.

Puharich and Cortes caught on fast. After rigorous experimentation like this, they proved, at least to themselves, that normally it hurts someone when you poke a knife into his eye, at least in a statistically significant number of cases, if the sample is large enough. Paranormal science marches on!

The scientific investigating techniques that are affirmed as exclusively valid by the cosmologists of human autonomy and neutral observation are impotent to handle the manifestations of the demonic. The questions that must be asked regarding the origins of such occult phenomena are denied from the start as being legitimate questions.[20]

OCCULT BONDAGE

Being healed from a dreaded disease or lingering illness is powerfully persuasive. Whether the healing is supernatural or psychological, when it is accomplished in an occult context the result is the same. Guy L. Playfair points out that the true purpose of the psychic surgeons is not just healing cataracts and kidney stones. Their primary mission is to influence people to adopt the occult faith. Playfair is himself an example: "Having experienced psychic surgery myself, I am forced to take the Spiritist faith seriously."[21] *Hence the purpose of psychic healing is philosophical-religious and not medical.*

For those who do not like the idea of spiritism, other ideas are put forth. Dr. LeShan believes in "the untapped human potential." Playfair looks forward to "advancing technology" and envisions the day "when psychic surgery will be performed by machines, anti-biomagnets, with which even complicated surgery will become an instantaneous do-it-yourself process."[22] After a while, one fears, such radionic-like technology will be dispensed with and most of our hospitals will serve the function of encouraging people to become mediums, as they do in some cultures in the Eastern world today.[23]

Those healed provide a good deal of favorable publicity for "the product," and they naturally become extremely interested in how the healing was brought about. As that knowledge usually carries with it an occult world view, many people gravitate toward or adopt such a perspective. And there is more involved than simply the decision to opt for a certain philosophy. There would seem to be a subtly forced progression from the physical aspects of the occult to the philosophical and religious. As we have seen, the healers themselves must accept and promote the occult world view in order to be effective.[24] There must be a harmony with the powers they use, a proper alignment, or attunement, to the spiritual forces that operate in the universe. Dr. Naegeli-Osjord comments, "It is my conviction that paranormal accomplishments of the healer demand a positive and harmonious attitude toward the environment and the cosmos.[25].

The Christian will look to God for his strength and healing and to God's wisdom if He chooses not to heal. We have discussed occult forms of "healing" in this book; believers in Christ must never forget that we can point the way to the most important healing: the spiritual healing of having one's sins forgiven. As Jesus noted, What will it profit a man to gain the whole world [including health] if he loses his own soul (Matthew 16:26)?

NOTES

1. Hans Holzer, *Beyond Medicine*, p. 45.
2. C. Norman Shealy, *Occult Medicine Can Save Your Life*, p. 186.
3. Kurt Koch, *Occult Bondage and Deliverance*, p. 30. Copyright 1970 by Kregel Publications. Used by permission.
4. Ibid., p. 33.
5. Ibid., pp. 33-34.
6. Kurt Koch, *Demonology Past and Present*, pp. 121, 129. Copyright 1973 by Kregel Publications. Used by permission.
7. Kurt Koch, *Satan's Devices*, p. 238.
8. Mircea Eliade, *Shamanism: Archaic Techniques of Ecstacy*, pp. 13, 20-23, 372-73.
9. Ibid., p. 22.
10. John Weldon and Zola Levitt, *The Transcendental Explosion*, chapter 4, appendix.

10. Koch, *Occult Bondage*, p. 42.
11. Koch, *Demonology*, p. 117; cf. pp. 112-17.
12. Ibid., p. 110.
13. Ibid., p. 116.
14. Koch, *Occult Bondage*, p. 40.
15. Koch, *Demonology*, p. 109.
16. George W. Meek, "Teaching People to Become Healers," in George W. Meek, ed., *Healers and the Healing Process*, p. 164.
17. Ibid., p. 165.
18. Ibid., p. 168.
19. Ibid., p. 164.
20. Gary K. North, *None Dare Call It Witchcraft*, pp. 144-49.
21. Guy L. Playfair, *The Unknown Power*, p. 124.
22. Ibid., p. 290.
23. Koch, *Occult Bondage*, p. 39.
24. Meek, pp. 85-87, 189-92.
25. Ibid., p. 87.

9

The Biblical View
of Sickness, Adversity,
and Healing

POSITIVE CONFESSION

Having examined the world of psychic healing, let us now briefly investigate Christian healing and some common misconceptions concerning it. (Those who wish to read a more exhaustive treatment should consult either *The Wall Street Gospel* by Joe Magliato or *From The Pinnacle of the Temple* by Charles Farah.) Unfortunately, there are those who teach that Christians should never be sick or poor or have problems; they should always be happy, healthy, and wealthy. At the least, they should "have abundance." That teaching is found among both the cults (e.g., The Way) and some Christian groups.

One common teaching is "positive confession" (similar to "the power of positive thinking"), that is, that we can control our lives and environment by not entertaining negative thoughts and by always "affirming" that which is good. Our minds control our life experiences and bring blessing or woe.

Although such teaching contains an element of truth, the extreme views taught today more or less simply repeat the Science of Mind ideas of Ernest

Holmes: Through positive affirmation, by uniting our mind with God's mind (the two become one), we can *divinely* control our environment and life. Holmes admittedly made up his own religion by combining elements of the occult and Eastern philosophy with the Bible.[1]

Another teaching is that no Christian ever need be sick; or if he does fall ill, he can be healed instantly by his attitude—that is, his "faith." Here faith becomes something of a "magical charm," something to control the divine will and force God to act. If we have the faith, then He *must* heal, regardless of His wishes. Thus, God is no longer the sovereign Lord doing as He pleases but is subject to man and his wishes.

Both of these teachings attempt the impossible—to bring heaven down to earth. Both ideas are symptoms of a deeper problem: lack of sound *biblical* teaching.

It appears that too many insufficiently taught people have become teachers, in spite of the fact that we are warned by God: "Let not many of you become teachers, my brethren, knowing that as such we shall incur a stricter judgment" (James 3:1). At the same time, some Christians are simply too undisciplined to make the effort to dig out the truths of Scripture. Hence, they propagate simplistic interpretations of Scripture that a more thorough study of God's Word would nullify. Diligent study is not easy and requires discipline and effort, but it is essential. In this day of biblical ignorance, false teachings, and proliferation of cults, simply reading the Bible like the morning newspaper is insufficient.

THE MIND AND SCRIPTURE

Some teach that we need ongoing revelations from God, or that the human mind itself, even redeemed, cannot really understand Scripture. Thus, experience must interpret Scripture. Yet Scripture itself tells us that apart from any additional divine revelations or experiences, if we have faith, we already have "the mind of Christ" (1 Corinthians 2:16). It is with our natural (that is, God-given) human mind that we are to understand Scripture. That is the consistent teaching throughout the Bible. We are never told that the Christian's mind is insufficient to understand spiritual things.

Would God stress loving Him with all our minds (Matthew 22:37); putting His laws into our minds (Hebrews 8:10; 10:16); having our minds renewed (Romans 12:2); being renewed in the spirit of our mind (Ephesians 4:23), and so on, if the mind were useless in spiritual matters?

However, it is true that the mind can be spiritually corrupted. Scripture refers to those who walk in the futility of their minds (Ephesians 4:17), men of corrupt or depraved mind (2 Timothy 3:8), those who "stirred up the minds" or caused division (Acts 14:2). "For there are many rebellious men, empty talkers and deceivers . . . who must be silenced because they are upsetting whole families [a common fruit of aberrant Christianity], teaching things they should not teach" (Titus 1:10-11). But Christians are to "conduct yourselves in a manner worthy of the gospel of Christ . . . standing firm in one spirit, with one mind striving together for the faith of the gospel; in no way alarmed by your opponents" (Philippians 1:27-28).

God places a premium on knowledge of His Word and proper doctrine because He knows false and harmful ideas, even heresy, will infiltrate the church, and that those ideas have consequences:

> For certain persons have crept in unnoticed, those who were long beforehand marked out for this condemnation, ungodly persons who turn the grace of

our God into licentiousness and deny our only Master and Lord, Jesus Christ (Jude 4).

Be on guard for yourselves and for all the flock, among which the Holy Spirit has made you overseers, to shepherd the church of God which He purchased with His own blood. I know that after my departure savage wolves will come in among you, not sparing the flock; and from among your own selves men will arise, speaking perverse things, to draw away the disciples after them. Therefore be on the alert, remembering that night and day for a period of three years I did not cease to admonish each one with tears (Acts 20:28-31).

But false prophets also arose among the people, just as there will also be false teachers among you, who will secretly introduce destructive heresies, even denying the Master who bought them, bringing swift destruction upon themselves. And many will follow their sensuality, and because of them the way of truth will be maligned; and in their greed they will exploit you with false words; their judgment from long ago is not idle, and their destruction is not asleep (2 Peter 2:1-3).

For there must also be factions among you, in order that those who are approved may have become evident among you (1 Corinthians 11:19).

THE VALUE OF DOCTRINE

Although some are teaching that doctrine has little or no value and is divisive (e.g., Witness Lee and The Local Church), that is not the biblical position. That *is* true for minor issues (e.g., food and drink), or issues upon which Scripture is not always entirely clear (e.g., eschatology). First Corinthians 1:10 is clear: unity is important. But, the unity spoken of there is not to be attained at the expense of key biblical truths—moral standards; doctrines of the nature of man, sin, God and salvation; or the authority of Scripture. It seems abundantly clear that doctrine is important to God:

Anyone who goes too far and does not abide in the teachings of Christ, does not have God; the one who abides in the teaching, he has both the Father and the Son (2 John 9-10).

Now I urge you, brethren, keep your eye on those who cause dissentions and hindrances contrary to the teaching which you learned, and turn away from them (Romans 16:17).

As I urged you upon my departure for Macedonia, remain on at Ephesus, in order that you may instruct certain men not to teach strange doctrines. . . . If anyone advocates a different doctrine, and does not agree with . . . the doctrine conforming to godliness, he is conceited and understands nothing (1 Timothy 1:3; 6:3-4).

Holding fast the faithful word which is in accordance with the teaching, that he may be able both to exhort in sound doctrine and to refute those who contradict. . . . But as for you, speak the things which are fitting for sound doctrine (Titus 1:9; 2:1).

Preach the Word; be ready in season and out of season; reprove, rebuke, exhort, with great patience and instruction. For the time will come when they will not endure sound doctrine (2 Timothy 4:2-3).

THE POWER OF FAITH

Having established the importance of biblical knowledge and doctrine, let us examine the biblical view of the teaching of "positive confession" and "totalistic healing." Such teachings are errors but not issues of heresy. God honors the preaching of the gospel, and those who teach those ideas can have real fruit in their ministries. Many are true Christian brothers with whom we can fellowship, although we should attempt to reason with them from the Scriptures. (However, it may not always be wise to fellowship at a church that teaches such ideas. Depending on the degree of extremes taught, more harm and spiritual impotence than good could result in such fellowships. Where there are extremes in one area, there may be in others.)

Let us briefly examine those ideas from the standpoint of Scripture. First, the basic issue in these teachings is that of *control*. Who is in control—God or man? If either positive confession or faith becomes an instrument whereby, if exercised properly, God *must* work, then the logical conclusion is that man can control God: it is man's positive confession that brings material possessions, friends, wealth; it is man's faith that brings healing. Essentially, what that is saying is that *mental processes* are or can become omnipotent: they can become "as God." We are thus back in the Garden of Eden: "You will be like God" (Genesis 3:5), or even before: "I will make myself like the Most High" (Isaiah 14:14; Ezekiel 28:1-10). The problems with such an idea are apparent.

There is another problem with such teaching. If positive confession *must* bring good, why does it fail so often? If negative ideas must always manifest a corresponding negative life situation, why do they not? David prayed in a state of acute depression, and his prayer was almost immediately answered (2 Samuel 15:30-32; 17:1-23). Elijah, Jonah, and others sincerely wished to die (1 Kings 19:4; Jonah 4:3), but they did not. Events from the lives of biblical characters repeatedly refute the idea that the mind has the power some attribute to it. Faith is important, and a person's faith in God is a part of healing as is evidenced in the Gospel accounts, but the crucial issue is God's will. Great faith will not force God to act where He does not choose to.

Biblically, faith is not a magic tool, but a trust in God. Whatever we pray for, or have faith for, must be in accordance with God's will, unless we would make ourselves God.

> And this is the confidence which we have before Him, that if we ask anything *according to His will*, He hears us. And if we know that He hears us in whatever we ask, we know that we have the requests which we have asked from Him (1 John 5:14-15, italics added).

God, in His infinite wisdom, does as He pleases (Job 42:2). Do we always know what is best? We are not omniscient, are we? A wise man can rejoice that God does *not* always answer his prayers. *"If the Lord wills*, we shall live and also do this or that" (James 4:15, italics added).

HEALING IN THE ATONEMENT

Some base the teaching that Christians are never to be sick on the idea that the atonement of Christ brought physical healing *as well as* spiritual healing; we need only believe it. Their key verse is, "Surely our griefs [sicknesses] He Himself bore . . . by His scourging we are healed" (Isaiah 53:4-5). Matthew 8:16-17 and 1 Peter 2:24 are used as confirmation.

Let us examine those verses. 1 Peter 2:24 is a quote of Isaiah 53:4-5, which thus provides us with an understanding of how Peter interpreted that Old Testament verse. The key question is, What kind of healing is being referred to? Judging from its context, 1 Peter 2:24 must refer to spiritual healing, not freedom from illness. Kenneth S. Wuest, in *Word Studies in the Greek New Testament*, explains:

> The blood of Christ heals our sin in that He by one offering put away sin forever. There is no room here for the healing of illness through the blood of Jesus. The Cross was a purely judicial matter. One goes to a hospital when one is ill, and to a law court to take

care of legal matters. In the great law court of the universe, the Judge offers mercy on the basis of justice satisfied at the Cross. The matter of bodily illness is not mentioned in the context. Furthermore, the Greek word used here is not confined in its meaning to physical healing. In Luke 4:18 it refers to the alleviation of heartaches, and in Hebrews 12:13, to the rectifying of one's conduct. In Matthew 13:15, it means, "to bring about (one's) salvation." This passage cannot therefore be made to teach the erroneous doctrine that healing of the body is to be found in the atonement as salvation from sin is found at the Cross. The context in which the word is found clearly decides the meaning of the word here, not that of the healing of the body, but that of the salvation of the soul.[2]

Furthermore, even our spiritual healing, individually, was not brought to *full* completion at the cross: we still sin. Therefore, even if Isaiah 53:4 taught physical healing by the atonement, there would be no reason to expect physical healing to be total *in this life*, just as our spiritual healing is not total in this life.

Matthew 8:16-17 seems to indicate that Isaiah 53:4 is speaking of physical healing: "He . . . healed all who were ill in order that what was spoken through Isaiah the prophet might be fulfilled saying, 'He Himself took our infirmities, and carried away our diseases' " (Matthew 8:16-17).

There are problems, however, in using these verses to support the idea of healing in the atonement. Notice in Matthew 8:17 that the prophecy in Isaiah *was then fulfilled* ("might be fulfilled"). If it was completely fulfilled then, is it still being fulfilled today? Was not the prophecy intended to apply to Christ healing the people during His earthly ministry only, as evidence of His unique Messiahship? In other words, is the fulfillment of Isaiah 53:4 in the atonement or in the *Person* of Christ (in His death or in His earthly ministry?) Furthermore, when Matthew applies the fulfillment of what Christ was doing at that moment (healing all who were ill), the atonement had not yet occurred, so how can this reference to Isaiah 53:4 be used to teach that the atonement itself brings healing? If Christ was healing before His death, His death could not be the cause of the healing.

So we see that Isaiah 53:4-5 can refer to different *aspects* of healing: physical (during Christ's earthly ministry) and spiritual. We can accept both meanings of the verse because the Hebrew word for "heal" (*napha*) used in Isaiah 53 has a variety of meanings. Many other Old Testament references to *napha* clearly do not indicate physical healing (e.g., 2 Chronicles 7:14; Psalm 107:20, 147:3; Jeremiah 3:22; Hosea 14:4). Thus we see the verses in Isaiah, Matthew, and Peter cannot be used to teach that Christians, because of the atonement, need never be sick.

CHRIST'S EXAMPLE

If God desires none to be ill, what of those whom Jesus passed by and did not heal? In John 5:3 there were a *multitude* of sick, blind, lame, and withered. Jesus often selected just one to heal, as He did in John 9, but He could have healed many more. Did the Savior possibly want some to remain sick? Why did He never say to the multitudes, "Have faith and you will *all* be healed"? The issue appears to be one of His choice. He healed those He wished to heal. If Jesus, who had all power and perfect faith, did not heal all, how can it be claimed today that He has changed His mind and that no one ever need be sick?

Which healer today, anywhere, will claim his healing ministry even approaches the quality of Jesus' healing ministry which was, as we have just seen, limited? Even if we have all faith, could we do better? The idea that healing is always dependent upon the amount of our faith, is contradicted by Scripture. If the atonement alone had physically healed believers (irrespective of faith to be healed), no sickness should occur or continue as sickness after the cross. "By His scourging you *are* [meaning "have been"] healed." If simple faith is required, why does it not still work? *All* Christians have been given faith ("God has allotted to each a measure of faith" Romans 12:3). Where in Scripture is *more* faith a requirement for healing?

SIN AND SICKNESS

Some will agree that the atonement dealt with the problem of sin but will say that since sin is the root of sickness, faith is the cure. In 1 Corinthians 11:30 we see that many Christians were "weak and sick" and some had died from the sickness. But Paul did not exhort those sick simply to *have more faith* but to judge themselves properly (spiritually). Obviously, faith was not a cure-all.

Also, it is obvious that some very godly Christians have been sick, and great faith on their part has not cured them. The great faith and prayers of hundreds of others for them has not cured them either. We must realize that healing is God's sovereign prerogative. Sometimes He heals; often He does not. A faith healer may tell you to believe and you *will* be healed, and you may truly believe, but you may not be healed. Even if you "feel" you have been healed, "cures" by religious suggestion should not be mistaken for the work of the Holy Spirit.

JAMES 5:13-18

The prayer in James 5 is a general principle, which, incidentally, depends on the elders' faith (v. 14), not the sick person's. Since (so far as we know) it did not work, at least physically, for Timothy, Paul, Epaphroditus and others, it is obviously not a magical formula.

Merrill F. Unger suggests that "the prayer of faith" was not universally given but "is only given when God's purpose is determined in each case, and such prayer is offered in God's will."[3] In other words, once the elders determined it was God's will to heal the person, "the prayer of faith" was given, and God healed. If the instructions of the verse are to be obeyed, the fact that the *elders* are to be called upon demands the meeting be in a local body where the elders would be likely to know the individual personally, which might be useful in determining God's will. For example, is the illness related to sin? Does the person need a life-saving "lesson" about overwork? It would seem, therefore, that these verses do not apply to so-called "miracle healing" services.

> The proper situation for praying for the sick to be healed, therefore, is not in a public healing campaign where the evangelistic faith healer knows little or nothing of those who come in a "healing line," but in the privacy and intimate fellowship of a local church situation. The observance of this directive alone would rule out public healing campaigns with their high pressure methods and Christ-dishonoring commercialism, because of which the career of so many faith-healers has been tarnished and Scriptural healing brought into disrepute.[4]

There have been cases in which the instructions of James 5 have been followed and the person has not been healed. That can mean only one thing—God's will is the determinative factor:

> They have never been able to pray "the prayer of faith" to be healed (James 5:14-16), simply because it was not God's will for them to be healed. Accordingly, God never granted them, nor those who prayed for them, such a prayer of faith, which must always be in God's will to be answered by God with genuine physical healing.[5]

Finally, some of Dr. Unger's comments are worth repeating in full:

> For so-called "faith healing" to teach that it is always God's will to heal believers and to command "God in Jesus' name" is a Satanic snare, into which so many modern faith healers have fallen. It is an open door to "white magic," where despite the use of God's name and religious pretentions, the creature dares to make the Creator his lackey. By so doing, he captures the very essence of "magic," which is Satanic opposition of God's will and desire to be like God and use His power independent of Him (Isaiah 14:12-14; 2 Timothy 2:26). To accomplish such a misguided purpose, however innocent or sincere as it may be, is an open invitation for demonic deception and operation, and it is high time for all who seek physical healing to realize this peril. . . . Since healing in this age must always reckon upon the will of God in each individual case, and since it is not always God's will to heal immediately or even gradually when factors of chastening or testing, or refining, etc. are involved, he who possesses gifts of healing must also exercise the gift of discernment (1 Corinthians 12:10). It is not enough merely to have facility in prayer and endowment of faith to pray for the sick. One must be able to ascertain God's will in each case in order to pray "the prayer of faith" (James 5:15) according to God's will, for such a prayer in reality cannot be prayed on any other

basis, if it gets divine and not demonic results. The mistake of so many who practice faith healing today is to attempt to pray "the prayer of faith" apart from ascertaining God's will in each case, holding that such a procedure rules out real faith. But the erroneous assumption put into practice carries with it the following perils. It easily flouts the will of God, which for various reasons may not be to heal the sick believer prayed for. It disregards the Word of God which clearly teaches that God has many purposes in human infirmity and the sickness of His own. It exposes the faith healer to the snare of looking to himself and his faith rather than to God. It also exposes those who attend the ministry of the faith leader to the snare of looking to him and his faith rather than to God. It therefore tends to idolize God's servant and put him in the place of God, thus violating the first basic commandment of the eternal moral law of God (cf. Exodus 20:3-5).

More perilous still this insistence on the will of the faith healer, under the pious cloak of "the prayer of faith," constitutes an open invitation to demonic spirits to enlist in a program that essentially dovetails with Satan's purpose of aping and opposing God. This demonstrates how easy it is for the unwary or poorly taught man of God to fall a prey to demonic forces and slip inadvertently into the technique of white magic. In this sphere the religious trappings of unsound doctrine form a mask, under which evil spirits may work to effect healings. But these healings are spurious in the sense that they require a compensation—a psychic disturbance in exchange for a physical cure, delusion by a false doctrine and involvement in a cult in exchange for physical relief, or enslavement to some bondage of conscience that tends to be productive of fanaticism.[6]

A second interpretation of this passage is one that is rarely seen, but the argumentation for it is persuasive. Daniel R. Hayden believes the passage refers to emotional sickness (discouragement, depression) and not physical sickness. He shows that his view is linguistically possible and contextually and experientially more probable than the current view of physical healing. We shall summarize some of his arguments.

First, he notes that the thrust of the New Testament teaching to Christians is not physical healing but encouragement "to view their physical distresses as merely temporary in the working out of a greater spiritual benefit (cf. Rom. 8:18-25; 2 Cor. 4:16-18); and [that] spiritual maturity comes as believers allow the trials of life to develop in them a patient spirit (James 1:2-4)."[7]

Second, the word "sick" in James 5:14 comes from a Greek word meaning "to strengthen" with the prefix a ("not") attached, giving a meaning of "to be weak." Twenty times the word is used of *physical* weakness (the sick) and fourteen times of *spiritual* weakness.*

> The emphasis of the word is on "weakness"; but the context determines whether it is being used of physical weakness or spiritual weakness.[8]
>
> The point here is that [astheneo] is a word which is used in the Epistles primarily to describe a spiritually "weak" person, and therefore James 5:14 should be properly translated, "Is any *weak* among you?" The context would certainly be agreeable to this rendering.[9]

The word "sick" in James 5:15 is a different Greek word, *kamno*.

> The only other occurrence of [kamno] in the New Testament gives insight into its meaning. "For consider Him who has endured such hostility by sinners

---

*We have used the English equivalent for Hayden's Greek.

against Himself, so that you may not grow weary [kamno] and lose heart. You have not yet resisted to the point of shedding blood in your striving against sin" (Heb. 12:3-4).

Although the word [kamno] can carry the idea of physical illness, both Arndt and Gingrich and Thayer agree that its primary usage pertains to growing weary or becoming fatigued. . . . Many Christians have struggled with some besetting sin and have known the weariness that can come to the mind, especially when that sin touches the point of some weakness. To be "weary" in the spiritual battle is the sense of [kamno], and James says "the prayer offered in faith will restore the one who is weary.[10]

Hayden concludes that the ministry of the elders is "to pray for spiritual strengthening for those who are discouraged or depressed," which is in harmony with the promise offered in the verse itself.

The evident promise inherent in the phrase "the prayer offered in faith will restore the one who is sick" (5:15) is an ever-lurking embarrassment for many who have known failure in trying to apply this passage to the physically ill. "The prayer offered in faith" is a prayer prayed in the full realization that it is God's will to answer that prayer in the manner desired, yet it is a difficult thing to know for sure in any given circumstance whether it is God's will for a certain person to be healed. . . . On the other hand if the elder is to pray for victory over sin and for encouragement in the spiritual conflict for a "weak" and "weary" saint, then there is really no question concerning God's will. God is never pleased with sin and is therefore always ready to forgive and to strengthen the believer who comes to Him by faith. The Apostle Paul says, "But thanks be to God, who always leads us in His triumph in Christ" (2 Cor. 2:14). Consequently to see in James 5 a ministry of elder support for the spiritually "weak" and "weary" is considerably more consistent than seeing physical healing in response to "the prayer of faith" in every situation.[11]

Hayden sees the "anointing with oil" in light of other uses in Scripture (e.g., Luke 7:38, 46; Matthew 6:17), which never use it in conjunction with healing. The word indicates a common practice of "bestowing honor, refreshment and grooming."

> If James is speaking of a ministry to the "weak" and "weary" in their struggle with temptation, then "annointing him with oil" would be a well-understood means of refreshment and encouragement. Instead of dragging around in a disheartened and disheveled condition as a result of extreme discouragement, James suggests that the person should be uplifted in faith toward God as the elders applied the refreshing and honored "annointing with oil"[12]

Hayden also shows that the word "healed" in James 5:16 can be employed for spiritual healing of the heart. He cites the use of the same word in Hebrews 12:12-13, where it is applied to those who are weak and weary.

He also points out that in light of the existence of spiritual gifts of healings in the church when James wrote, it is noteworthy that this verse does not call for the gifted persons but for the elders, those whose ministry is primarily giving leadership to the church and support to the saints in their struggles.

> James tells the "weak" to call for the strong ("elders") that they may be strengthened through a spiritual ministry of prayer. Paul makes a similar appeal to the elders of the church when he says, "Brethren, even if a man is caught in any trespass, you who are spiritual, restore such a one in a spirit of gentleness" (Gal. 6:1). Certainly the fact that James calls for the "elders" is further evidence that he has a spiritual ministry in mind—not a healing of the physically sick.[13]

At the same time, Hayden observes there may be physical problems associated with spiritual struggles:

> In fact, in the opinion of this writer, the words and contextual thoughts of James 5 do not support the view that "sickness due to sin" is intended in the passage (although there does seem to be an allowance for certain physical ramifications as a part of the individual's problem). The emphasis of James is clearly on the emotional distress and spiritual exhaustion experienced by God's people in their deep struggle with temptation and their relentless battle with besetting sin. Deep emotional and psychological pressure will often manifest itself in physical ways as has been demonstrated in the study of psychosomatic illness, and in that sense there may be physical aspects to the problem spoken of by James.[14]

Finally a strong supporting argument is provided from James's choice of illustrations. Had James intended primarily physical healing, he perhaps used a less than relevant illustration.

> Finally there is a crowning effect in the illustration chosen by James to conclude his argument. His choice of Elijah (5:17-18) from among all the heroes of the faith is both deliberate and perceptive in that he most effectively pictures the possibility of effective prayer by a "weak" and "weary" saint.
>
> James refers to Elijah's prayer that it would not rain for three years and six months. While this prayer as such is not recorded in 1 Kings, it may have been made some way in connection with his pronouncement to Ahab about God's withholding of rain as His displeasure against Israel's sin (1 Kings 17:1). But why did James not refer to Elijah's dramatic prayer for the healing of the widow's son (1 Kings 17:17-24)? Surely James would have chosen that prayer if he were seeking to illustrate effective pray-

ing for physical healing. The fact that he chose the first incident demonstrates that he sought to picture fervent prayer in the midst of conflict with sin rather than a prayer ministry for the sick.

Furthermore the great prophet Elijah is as well known for his weakness as he is for his strength. When James says that Elijah was "a man with a nature like ours" (5:17), he is obviously referring to that one unforgettable event when the prophet became weary in his continued contest with the nation's sin. His discouragement turned to depression, and he fled in fear and cried out to God to take his life (1 Kings 19:1-5). Even great men of God are in need of God's special strengthening when they become weary in battle. This picturesque incident from the life of Elijah gives strong support to the view that James is referring to a spiritual ministry to the "weak" and "weary" rather than to a ministry of healing for the physically sick.[15]

The above two views of this passage indicate that, at the least, it cannot be taken as a cure-all formula for physical healing. The suggestions by Unger and Hayden make more sense than those of the positive confession/faith-principle movements.

POSITIVE SICKNESS

Physical illness and imperfection can be used by God for His glory (John 9:1-3). The perfections of eternity will not be brought into a sin-cursed world. If the book of Revelation promises that in heaven there will be no sickness, that does not imply that God wills it here. God tells us, "My thoughts are not your thoughts, neither are your ways My ways." They are as removed from ours as the heavens are the earth (Isaiah 55:8-9).

If that is true, it would be unwise for us to try to make God's ways become our ways. God can use pain and suffering for a higher purpose than our limited and rather fallen minds can comprehend. If He could not, then what would we do with the cross? If we believe God accomplished the redemption of the world through infinite pain and suffering at the cross, then obviously He can use illness for a higher purpose. Job wisely said: "Shall we indeed accept good from God and not accept adversity?" (Job 2:10).

Shall we, in our lives, deny God the opportunity of turning evil to good, pain to joy, and sometimes sin to righteousness? There are many who because of illness and adversity have had a Christlike character built into them—rare, beauteous, and God-glorifying—which perhaps was not possible any other way. Even Jesus learned obedience through the things He suffered (Hebrews 5:8). In all eternity there is only one time when God can show us the constancy of His love and care for us in the midst of trial, suffering, adversity, agony, illness, loss. That time is now.

Many have discovered what God has done in their lives through suffering, and are grateful for it. Should Christians deny Him who willingly went to the cross the opportunity of adding a dimension of love, or wisdom, or character, or whatever, to their lives, *through suffering*, if it be His will? Or should Christians deny Him His right, and maintain that not even infinite wisdom and love could have a purpose in pain and suffering? How meager is our concept of the infinite God. Will our pride interfere with His purposes?

In Matthew 25:44 we read that even Jesus Himself expected sickness and difficulties among believers: "Lord, when did we see you hungry, or thirsty, or a stranger, or naked, or *sick*, or in prison . . .?" (italics added). There is abundant scriptural testimony to illness among men of great faith:

Exodus 4:11: "who has made him . . . [man] dumb or deaf, or seeing or blind? Is it not I, the LORD?"

2 Kings 13:14: Elisha was sick unto death.

Ezekiel 34:16: says the sick will be strengthened, not necessarily cured

Daniel 8:27: Daniel's "sickness for days" from God's vision.

John 11:2: Lazarus was sick unto death.

Acts 9:36-37: Dorcas was sick unto death.

Galatians 4:13-15: Paul had a "bodily illness."

Philippians 2:25-30: Epaphroditus was sick.

1 Timothy 5:23: Timothy's stomach illness

2 Timothy 4:20: Trophimus was left sick at Miletus.

James 5:14: Expects sickness and states only some sickness is from sin (note the "if").

Who of the above was not a person of great faith? Clearly the idea that no believer should ever be sick is unbiblical. Let us not be led astray by unbiblical definitions of faith and healing such as that of John Robert Stevens, founder of an aberrant Christian sect, The Church of the Living Word (The Walk):

> When you have certain aches and pains, and there-fore you come to the conclusion you are sick, you pray and ask the Lord to heal sickness. From that point on there must be another kind of knowledge that comes to bear on the situation [mystical/irrational and unbiblical "faith"]. If the pain persists and you conclude by this evidence that you are not healed, then you are coming to a conclusion based on your sense of feeling rather than on God's prom-ise. The revelation that comes to the inner man is based on God's Word, which seems to be completely unreasonable because it goes against the evidence of the senses. It goes against what you see or feel or hear. It goes against everything that is normally used to arrive at knowledge through scientific in-quiry. *You must refuse to consider scientific evi-*

*dence or accept it as reality, for God's Word is true:
with His stripes we are healed (Isaiah 53:5). As you
stand upon that promise in God's Word, it becomes
the reality, and soon you will base every situation
upon another kind of knowledge.*[16]

*God does not honor prayers of irrational faith
based upon false interpretations of His Word.*

THE FRUIT OF FALSE DOCTRINES OF HEALING

Some Christians are bitter or doubt their faith because they are sick and not healed. Others have
foregone treatment or withheld it from their loved
ones because they were told they were healed.
While they "kept the faith," they have remained ill or
died. Those who teach false doctrines of healing re-
spond to such situations by saying that God was just
testing their faith or that their faith was not strong or
genuine enough. The victim never wins; the healer
or the false doctrine always has an "answer" for
failure.

How much damage has been done by those who
preach such things in the name of Christ, despite
their good intentions? No wonder James warns that
not many of us are to become teachers of the Word,
knowing we shall incur a stricter judgment. "For we
all stumble in many ways" (James 3:1-2). We are to
be diligent to present ourselves "approved to God as
a workman who does not need to be ashamed, han-
dling accurately the word of truth" (2 Timothy 2:15).

THE CHRISTIAN'S RESPONSE TO SUFFERING

The idea that no Christian should ever suffer is
erroneous. The Bible repeatedly acknowledges that
Christians will suffer and have difficulties.

Therefore do not be anxious for tomorrow; for tomorrow will care for itself. Each day has enough trouble
of its own (Matthew 6:34).

In this you greatly rejoice, even though now for a
little while, if necessary, you have been distressed
by various trials. . . . Beloved, do not be surprised at
the fiery ordeal among you, which comes upon you
for your testing, as though some strange thing were
happening to you; but to the degree that you share
the sufferings of Christ, keep on rejoicing; so that
also at the revelation of His glory, you may rejoice
with exultation. If you are reviled for the name of
Christ, you are blessed, because the Spirit of glory
and of God rests upon you. By no means let any of
you suffer as a murderer, or thief, or evildoer, or a
troublesome meddler; but if anyone suffers as a
Christian, let him not feel ashamed, but in that
name let him glorify God. . . . Therefore, let those
also who suffer according to the will of God entrust
their souls to a faithful Creator in doing what is right
(1 Peter 1:6, 4:12-16, 19).

All the positive confession of faith in the world will
not stop our suffering unless it be God's will. "Positive confession" did not work for Paul—he accepted
the necessity of his suffering. Among men, no
greater example of Christian living is provided than
by the apostle Paul. But as mature as he was, as full
of faith as he was, he "suffered the loss of all things"
(Philippians 3:7-8) and learned to be content while
living in poverty, going hungry, and suffering need
(2 Corinthians 11:9, Philippians 4:12). Paul said,
"Now I rejoice in my sufferings for your sake" (Colossians 1:24). He said we are "fellow heirs with Christ,
if indeed we suffer with Him" (Romans 8:17) and that
"the sufferings of Christ are ours in abundance"
(2 Corinthians 1:5). Three times Paul entreated the
Lord to remove an affliction that made him "weak,"
and God said no three times. Did Paul have insufficient faith, was he unenlightened about "positive
confession," or did he come to see suffering as God's
gracious working in his life (2 Corinthians 12:7-10)? A

reading of 2 Corinthians 11:23-29 and James 4 and 5 should quell forever the "prosperity doctrines."

What about Christian healing then? Doesn't God heal? He did in the Old Testament, and He did in the New Testament. It is likely then that he does so today. In light of 1 Corinthians 12, it is difficult to believe that God is no longer gifting His church as He sees fit. We believe that in the area of healing, the important issue is our attitude and relationship to God. If we are physically sick, God can be trusted just the same as if we are physically well. Let us continue growing and trusting as long as we have breath to survive. We can, if we choose, ask Him to heal us. We can request others to pray. And we can leave the answer to His infinite wisdom rather than to man's limited knowledge. If He does not heal us, we should not allow others to make us feel guilty or depressed over our "lack of faith." We are to live our lives in sincerity before God, and no man has the right to judge our faith.

NOTES

1. *Science of Mind*, February 1979, p. 40. See John Weldon, *A Critical Encyclopedia of Religious Cults.*
2. Kenneth S. Wuest, *Acts to Ephesians*, in Word Studies in the Greek New Testament, 2:70.
3. Merrill F. Unger, "Divine Healing," p. 242. Used by permission.
4. Ibid.
5. Ibid., p. 244.
6. Ibid., pp. 239, 241-42.
7. D. R. Hayden, "Calling the Elders to Pray," p. 259. Used by permission.
8. Ibid., p. 260.
9. Ibid.

10. Ibid.
11. Ibid., pp. 263-64.
12. Ibid., p. 265.
13. Ibid., p. 262.
14. Ibid., p. 263.
15. Ibid., p. 265.
16. John Robert Stevens, *Sparks from the Altar*, p. 44.

10

Conclusion

We have attempted to examine the major problems associated with psychic or occult healing. We have looked at psychic diagnosis and noted with few exceptions its general ineffectiveness as well as potential dangers for misdiagnosis.

We saw that when certain devices are used to diagnose or heal, the real power is resident in the healer rather than in a supposedly new technology of psychic instrumentation.

In an examination of five prominent psychic healers, we noted that they all hold a nonbiblical world view. We saw that their particular methodology in itself was impotent in healing (apart from a possible psychological impact) but that the important factor was the occultic power of the healer. Thus, people not involved with the occult cannot heal psychically; only occultists can. This rebuts the basic parapsychological teaching that everyone has natural, latent healing abilities. Genuine psychic healing uses demonic energy.

Our examination of psychic surgery brought out its similarity to ancient shamanistic healing. Modern cases simply incorporate modern cultural variables.

Psychic surgery is thus a "twentieth-century medical" form of Shamanistic healing. Typically, the "surgeon" has no medical background and often acknowledges his dependence on trance states through which his "spirit doctors" work. Their power is not latent, and their effectiveness is questionable.

Many features are common to psychic diagnosis, healing, and surgery. Fraud is prevalent, particularly in psychic surgery. Another feature is lack of documentation of their effectiveness. Perhaps the lowest common denominator is that of spiritism. Psychic healers universally depend upon the spirits to do their healing work. If the spirits are absent the healers are powerless. Finally, we noticed a semantic subterfuge—spirits operating under neutral concepts ("the higher self," etc).

Much of what is claimed as healing is probably the result of psychological rather than psychic or supernatural factors. Nevertheless, a kind of Faustian bargain takes place. Those who seek out psychic healers often come into occult bondage and become insulated against the gospel. Often those who seek physical healing in a psychic environment not only are not healed, but they are afflicted spiritually. And, of course, the very time spent with a psychic healer in long, drawn out treatments can allow the illness to reach a more serious level. Psychic healing offers one poor hope physically and no hope spiritually.

Because of the Fall, man is naturally disposed to physical failings. Often his own poor choices in lifestyle compound the problem. As we might expect, God's enemy, Satan, has engineered a strategy for soothing man's physical concerns. But no one can bargain with God. He cannot and will not be forced to heal against His will.

Too often, some within the church have been

taken in by a cultural malaise and have introduced the grandiose claims of positive thinking as a biblical mandate. However, positivism and "faith" cannot guarantee freedom from illness or insure success. God heals and abundantly blesses those whom He chooses according to His own purposes. Maturity in Christ allows an infinitely wise Father the right to do with His children as He sees fit. True faith provides His children with contentment as they rest in His care and in the knowledge that He will indeed do what is best.

Moody Press, a ministry of the Moody Bible Institute, is designed for education, evangelization, and edification. If we may assist you in knowing more about Christ and the Christian life, please write us without obligation: Moody Press, c/o MLM, Chicago, Illinois 60610.

BIBLIOGRAPHY

BOOKS

Academy of Parapsychology and Medicine. *The Dimensions of Healing: A Symposium.* Denver: Academy of Parapsychology and Medicine, 1972.

————. *The Varieties of Healing Experience.* Denver: Academy of Parapsychology and Medicine, 1971.

Ash, Michael. *The Handbook of Natural Healing.* Launceston, UK: Camspress, 1977.

Association for Research and Enlightenment. *The Early Christian Epoch.* Edgar Cayce Readings, vol. 6. Virginia Beach, Va.: Association for Research and Enlightenment, 1976.

————. *The Healing Mechanism: An Adventure in Consciousness.* 8th Annual Medical Symposium sponsored by ARE and Edgar Cayce Foundation. Phoenix, Az.: Association for Research and Enlightenment, 1975.

————. *New Horizons in Healing.* 7th Annual Medical Symposium. Phoenix, Az.: Association for Research and Enlightenment, 1974.

————. *A Symposium on Mind-Body Relationships in the Disease Process.* 5th Annual Medical Symposium. Phoenix, Az.: Association for Research and Enlightenment, 1972.

————. *A Symposium on the Varieties of Healing.* 6th Annual Medical Symposium. Phoenix, Az.: Association for Research and Enlightenment, 1973.

Baker, Douglas. *Esoteric Healing.* Vols. 1 and 2. Essendon Herts, England: Douglas Baker, 1975, 1976.

Barnothy, Madeleine F., ed. *Biological Effects of Magnetic Fields.* 2 vols. New York: Plenum, 1969.

Beasley, Victor. *Dimensions of Electro-Vibratory*

Phenomena. Boulder Creek, Calif.: U. of the Trees, 1975.

Berkeley Holistic Health Center. *The Holistic Health Handbook*. Berkeley, Calif.: And/Or, 1978.

Bishop, George. *Faith Healing–God or Fraud?* Los Angeles: Shergourne, 1976.

Bjornstad, James. *Twentieth Century Prophecy: Jean Dixon–Edgar Cayce*. Minneapolis: Bethany Fellowship, 1969.

Blair, Lawrence. *Rhythms of Vision*. New York: Schocken, 1976.

Boettner, Loraine. *Roman Catholicism*. Philadelphia: Presbyterian & Reformed, 1973.

Bowles, Norma, and Hynds, Fran. *PsiSearch*. New York: Harper & Row, 1973.

Boyd, Doug. *Rolling Thunder*. New York: Dell, 1974.

Braid, James. *Neurypnology, or, The Rationale of Nervous Sleep in Relation with Animal Magnetism*. 1843. Reprint. New York: Arno, 1975.

Brena, Stephen F. *Yoga and Medicine*. New York: Penguin, 1976.

Brown, Slater. *The Heyday of Spiritualism*. New York: Pocket, 1972.

Buranelli, Vincent. *The Wizard from Vienna*. New York: Coward, 1975.

Burroughs, Stanley. *Healing for the Age of Enlightenment*. Kailua, Hawaii: Stanley Burroughs, 1976.

Carrington, Hereward. *Your Psychic Powers and How to Develop Them*. Van Nuys, Calif.: Newcastle, 1975.

Cayce, Edgar E., and Cayce, Hugh L. *The Outer Limits of Edgar Cayce's Power*. New York: Harper & Row, 1973.

Cocciardi, Carol, ed. *The Psychic Yellow Pages*. Saratoga, Calif.: Out of the Sky, 1977.

Coddington, Mary. *In Search of the Healing Energy.* New York: Warner Destiny, 1978.

deSmedt, Evelyn. *Lifearts: A Practical Guide to Total Being–New Medicine and Ancient Wisdom.* New York: St. Martin, 1977.

Douglas, Alfred. *Extra-Sensory Powers: A Century of Psychical Research.* New York: Overlook, 1977.

Ebon, Martin, ed. *Parapsychology.* New York: New American Library, 1978.

———. *The Satan Trap: Dangers of the Occult.* Garden City, N.Y.: Doubleday, 1976.

Eden, Jerome. *Animal Magnetism and the Life Energy.* Hicksville, N.Y.: Exposition, 1974.

Eliade, Mircea. *From Medicine Men to Muhammad.* New York: Harper & Row, 1967.

———. *Shamanism: Archaic Techniques of Ecstacy.* Translated by Willard R. Trask. Bollinger Series LXXVI. Princeton, N.J.: Princeton U., 1972.

Ernest, Victor. *I Talked with Spirits.* Wheaton, Ill.: Tyndale, 1971.

Farah, Charles. *The Pinnacle of the Temple.* Plainfield, N.J.: Logos, 1979.

Fodor, Nandor. *An Encyclopaedia of Psychic Science.* Secaucus, N.J.: Citadel, 1974.

Fuller, John G. *Arigo: Surgeon of the Rusty Knife.* New York: Pocket, 1975.

Furst, Jeffrey. *Edgar Cayce's Story of Jesus.* New York: Coward-McCann, 1970.

Gallimore, J. G. *The Handbook of Unusual Energies.* Mokelumne Hill, Calif.: Health Research, 1976.

Garrison, Omar V. *Medical Astrology.* New York: Warner, 1973.

Gasson, Raphael. *The Challenging Counterfeit.* Plainfield, N.J.: Logos, 1970.

Glass, Justine. *Witchcraft–The Sixth Sense.* Hollywood, Calif.: Wilshire, 1974.

Grant, Robert, ed. *Gnosticism: A Sourcebook of Heretical Writings from the Early Christian Period.* New York: AMS Harper, 1961.

Gregory, William. *Animal Magnetism: Or, Mesmerism and Its Phenomena.* 5th ed. 1909. Reprint. New York: Arno, 1975.

Gris, Henry, and Dick, William. *The New Soviet Psychic Discoveries.* Englewood Cliffs, N.J.: Prentice-Hall, 1978.

Hammond, David. *The Search for Psychic Power.* New York: Bantam, 1975.

Hammond, Sally. *We Are All Healers.* New York: Harper & Row, 1973.

Harner, Michael, ed. *Hallucinogens and Shamanism.* New York: Oxford U., 1973.

Hastings, Arthur; Fadiman, James; and Gordon, James, eds. *Health for the Whole Person—The Complete Guide to Holistic Medicine.* Boulder, Colo.: Westview, 1980.

Heline, Corrine. *Healing and Regeneration Through Color.* La Canada, Calif.: New Age, 1976.

Hills, Christopher. *Supersensonics.* Boulder Creek, Calif.: U. of the Trees, 1975.

Hodges, Doris M. *Healing Stones.* Perry, Iowa: Kiawatha, 1961.

Holmes, Fenwicke. *Ernest Holmes: His Life and Times.* New York: Dodd, Mead, 1970.

Holzer, Hans. *Beyond Medicine.* New York: Ballantine, 1974.

———. *The Truth About Witchcraft.* New York: Pocket, 1971.

Hunther, Bernard. *Energy Ecstasy and Your Seven Vital Chakras.* Los Angeles: Guild of Tutors, 1978.

Jansky, Robert C. *Modern Medical Astrology.* Van Nuys, Calif.: Astro-Analytics, 1973.

Jayne, Walter A., M.D. *The Healing Gods of Ancient Civilizations.* New Hyde Park, N.Y.: University, 1962.

Karagulla, Shafica, M.D. *Breakthrough to Creativity.* Santa Monica, Calif.: DeVorss, 1967.

Kaslof, Leslie J., ed. *Wholistic Dimensions in Healing: A Resource Guide.* Garden City, N.Y.: Doubleday, 1978.

Keller, Helen. *My Religion.* New York: Swedenborg, 1974.

Kingston, Jeremy. *Healing Without Medicine.* London: Aldus, 1975.

Kittel, Gerhard, ed. *Theological Dictionary of the New Testament.* 9 vols. Grand Rapids: Eerdmans, 1978.

Koch, Kurt. *Between Christ and Satan.* Grand Rapids: Kregel, 1962.

———. *Christian Counseling and Occultism.* Grand Rapids: Kregel, 1965.

———. *Demonology, Past and Present.* Grand Rapids: Kregel, 1973.

———. *The Devil's Alphabet.* Grand Rapids: Kregel, 1969.

———. *Occult Bondage and Deliverance.* Grand Rapids: Kregel, 1970.

———. *Satan's Devices.* Grand Rapids: Kregel, 1978.

Kreiger, Dolores. *The Therapeutic Touch.* Englewood Cliffs, N.J.: Prentice-Hall, 1979.

Krippner, Stanley, and Villoldo, Alberto. *The Realms of Healing.* Millbrae, Calif.: Celestial Arts, 1976.

Lande, Nathaniel. *Mindstyles, Lifestyles.* Los Angeles: Price Stern, 1976.

LaPatra, Jack. *Healing–The Coming Revolution in Holistic Medicine.* New York: McGraw-Hill, San Francisco Book, 1978.

Leek, Sybil. *My Life in Astrology.* Englewood Cliffs, N.J.: Prentice Hall, 1972.

LeShan, Lawrence. *The Medium, the Mystic, and the Physicist.* New York: Ballantine, Esalen, 1975.

Long, Max Freedom. *The Secret Science Behind Miracles*. Santa Monica, Calif.: DeVorss, 1948.

Magliato, Joe. *The Wall Street Gospel*. Irvine, Calif.: Harvest House, 1981.

Martin, Walter K. *Kingdom of the Cults*. Minneapolis: Bethany Fellowship, 1968.

―――. *The Maze of Mormonism*. Santa Ana, Calif.: Vision House, 1978.

―――. *The New Cults*. Santa Ana, Calif.: Vision House, 1980.

McConkie, Bruce. *Doctrinal New Testament Commentary*. Salt Lake City, Ut.: Bookcraft, 1976.

―――. *Mormon Doctrine*. Salt Lake City, Ut.: Bookcraft, 1977.

McGarey, William A. *Acupuncture and Body Energies*. Phoenix, Az.: Gabriel, 1974.

Meek, George W., ed. *Healers and the Healing Process*. Wheaton, Ill.: Theosophical Pub., 1977.

Millard, Joseph. *Edgar Cayce, Man of Miracles*. Cedar Knolls, N.J.: Wehman, 1963.

Miller, Paul. *Born to Heal–A Biography of Harry Edwards*. London: Spiritualist, n.d.

Mishlove, Jeffrey. *The Roots of Consciousness*. New York: Random House, 1975.

Mitchell, Edgar, and White, John, eds. *Psychic Exploration: A Challenge for Science*. New York: Putnam, 1976.

Montgomery, John, ed. *Demon Possession*. Minneapolis: Bethany Fellowship, 1975.

Montgomery, John. *Principalities and Power*. Minneapolis: Bethany Fellowship, 1973.

Montgomery, Ruth. *Born to Heal*. New York: Popular Library, 1974.

―――. *A Search for the Truth*. New York: Morrow, 1967.

Moss, Thelma. *The Probability of the Impossible*. New York: New American Library, 1975.

Motoyama, Hiroshi. *The Non-Physical in the Correlation Between Mind and Body.* Tokyo: Institute of Religious Psychology, 1972.

———. *Tony Agpaoa's Psychic Surgery and Its Mechanism.* Tokyo: Institute of Religious Psychology, 1978.

Murphet, Howard. *Sai Baba, Man of Miracles.* New York: Samuel Weiser, 1976.

Nolen, William A. *Healing: A Doctor in Search of a Miracle.* New York: Random, 1974.

North, Gary K. *None Dare Call It Witchcraft.* New Rochelle, N.Y.: Arlington House, 1976.

Ohsawa, George. *Acupuncture and the Philosophy of the Far East.* Boston: Tao, 1973.

Oken, Alan. *Astrology: Evolution and Revolution.* New York: Bantam, 1976.

Ornstein, Dolph, M.D. *Medicine Today, Healing Tomorrow.* Millbrae, Calif.: Celestial Arts, 1976.

Ostrander, Sheila, and Schroeder, Lynn. *The ESP Papers.* New York: Bantam, 1976.

Oteri, Laura, ed. *Quantum Physics and Parapsychology: Proceedings.* Proceedings of international conference in Geneva, Switzerland, August 26-27, 1974. New York: Parapsychology Foundation, 1975.

Ouseley, S. G. J. *The Power of the Rays.* London: Fowler, 1951.

———. *The Science of the Aura.* London: Fowler, 1949.

Oyle, Irving. *The Healing Mind.* Millbrae, Calif.: Celestial Arts, 1976.

———. *Magic, Mysticism, and Modern Medicine.* Millbrae, Calif.: Celestial Arts, 1976.

Playfair, Guy L. *The Unknown Power.* New York: Simon & Schuster, 1975.

Popenoe, Cris, ed. *Books for Inner Development: The Yes! Bookshop Guide.* New York: Random, 1976.

————. *Wellness*. Washington, D.C.: Yes!, 1977.

Presman, A. S. *Electromagnetic Fields and Life*. New York: Plenum, 1970.

Regush, Nicholas M. *The Human Aura*. New York: Berkeley, 1974.

Reilly, Harold J., and Brod, Ruth H. *The Edgar Cayce Handbook for Health Through Drugless Therapy*. New York: MacMillan, 1975.

Reisser, Paul, and Weldon, John. *The New Healers*. Unpublished manuscript.

Rhine, Louisa E. *PSI: What Is It?* New York: Harper & Row, 1975.

Rinpoche, V. Rechung. *Tibetan Medicine*. Berkeley, Calif.: U. of Calif., 1976.

Roberts, Jane. *The Seth Material*. New York: Bantam, 1976.

Rose, Ronald H. *Primitive Psychic Power*, New York: New American Library, 1956.

Sannella, Lee. *Kundalini: Transcendence or Psychosis?* Berkeley, Calif: Intergalactic, 1975.

Seabrook, William. *Witchcraft: Its Power in the World Today*. New York: Lancer, 1968.

Sereda, Lynn. *Outward Bound–The Spiritual Basis of the New Self-Integrative Therapies*. Vancouver, B.C.: Light-House, 1977.

Shah, Idries. *Oriental Magic*. New York: Dutton, 1972.

Shealy, C. Norman. *Occult Medicine Can Save Your Life*. New York: Bantam, 1977.

Sherman, Harold. *Wonder Healers of the Philippines*. Santa Monica, Calif.: DeVorss, 1974.

————. *Your Power to Heal*. Greenwich, Conn.: Fawcett World, 1976.

Solomon, Paul. *A Healing Conciousness*. Virginia Beach, Va.: Master's, 1978.

————. *The Paul Solomon Tapes*. Virginia Beach, Va.: Fellowship of the Inner Light, 1974.

Spragget, Allan. *Ross Peterson: The New Edgar Cayce*. New York: Doubleday, 1977.

Stanford, Ray. *What Your Aura Tells Me*. Garden City, NY: Doubleday, 1977.

Stapleton, Ruth Carter. *Experiencing Inner Healing*. Waco, Tex.: Word, 1977.

Steiner, Lee R. *Psychic Self-Healing for Psychological Problems*. Englewood Cliffs, N.J.: Prentice Hall, 1977.

Stevens, John Robert. *Sparks from the Altar*. North Hollywood, Calif.: Living Word, 1977.

Sugrue, Thomas. *Stranger in the Earth*. New York: Paperback Lib., 1971.

———. *There Is a River*. New York: Dell, 1970.

Tansley, David. *Radionics and the Subtle Anatomy of Man*. Bradford, England: Health Science, 1972.

Tart, Charles. *PSI: Scientific Studies of the Psychic Realm*. New York: Dutton, 1977.

Tenney, Merrill, C., ed. *Zondervan Pictorial Encyclopedia of the Bible*. 5 vols. Grand Rapids: Zondervan, 1977.

Theosophical Research Centre. *The Mystery of Healing*. Wheaton, Ill.: Theosophical Pub., 1958.

Thomas, Keith. *Religion and the Decline of Magic*. New York: Scribners, 1971.

Unger, Merrill F. *Demons in the World Today*. Wheaton, Ill.: Tyndale, 1972.

Valentine, Tom. *Psychic Surgery*. Chicago: Regnery, 1973.

Valiente, Doreen. *A.B.C. of Witchcraft*. New York: St. Martin's, 1973.

Wallace, Amy, and Henkin, Bill. *The Psychic Healing Book*. New York; Delacorte, 1978.

Warfield, Benjamin B. *Counterfeit Miracles*. Carlisle, Pa.: Banner of Truth, 1976.

Warnke, Mike, and Balsiger, Dave. *The Satan-Seller*. Plainfield, N.J.: Logos, 1972.

Watson, Lyall. *Super Nature.* New York: Bantam, 1974.

Weatherhead, Leslie D. *Psychology, Religion and Healing.* Nashville: Abingdon, 1951.

Weingarten, Henry. *A Modern Introduction to Astrology.* New York: ASI Pub., 1974.

Weldon, John. *Is There Life After Death?* Irvine, Calif.: Harvest House, 1977.

Weldon, John, and Levitt, Zola. *Encounters with UFOs.* Irvine, Calif.: Harvest House, 1975.

————. *The Transcendental Explosion.* Irvine, Calif.: Harvest House, 1977.

West, O. J. *Eleven Lourdes Miracles.* London: Duckworth, 1957.

Westlake, Aubrey T. *The Pattern of Health.* Boulder, Colo.: Shambhala, 1973.

White, John, ed. *Frontiers of Consciousness.* Chicago: Avon, 1975.

Wilson, Clifford, and Weldon, John. *1980s: Decade of Shock.* San Diego: Master, 1980.

————. *Occult Shock and Psychic Forces.* San Diego: Master, 1980.

Wilson, Colin. *The Occult.* New York: Random House, 1973.

Wolman, Benjamin B., et al, eds. *Handbook of Parapsychology.* New York: Van Nostrand Reinhold, 1977.

Worrall, Ambrose A., and Worrall, Olga N. *Explore Your Psychic World.* New York: Harper & Row, 1970.

————. *The Gift of Healing.* New York: Harper & Row, 1965.

Wuest, Kenneth S. *Acts to Ephesians.* Word Studies in the Greek New Testament, vol. 2. Grand Rapids: Eerdmans, 1958.

Zaretsky, Irving I., and Leone, Mark P., eds. *Reli-*

gious Movements in Contemporary America. Princeton, N.J.: Princeton U., 1974.

PERIODICALS

American Society of Psychical Research Journal. 1970-79.

ARE (Association for Research and Enlightenment) News, July 1977.

ARE Journals. 1976-79.

Bartlett, Laile E. "New Revelations about Psychic Phenomena." Reader's Digest, August 1977, p. 86.

Brain-Mind Bulletin, 9 March 1978.

The Christian Parapsychologist 3, no. 2.

Fadiman, James. "The Prime Cause of Healing." Journal of Holistic Health, 1977, p. 16.

Foreward 3, no. 2. A publication of the Christian Research Institute, 1550 S. Anaheim Blvd., Suite C., Anaheim, CA 92805.

Hammond, Sally. "What the Healers Say: A Survey of Healers in Britain." Psychic, July-August 1973, p. 14.

Hayden, D.R. "Calling the Elders to Pray." Bibliotheca Sacra, July-September 1981, p. 259.

Human Behavior. January 1977, pp. 39-40; September 1977, pp. 18-27.

Journal of Holistic Health. Association for Holistic Health/Mandala Society. 1975-76, 1977, 1978, 1979.

Kreiger, Dolores. "Therapeutic Touch and Healing Energies from Laying on of Hands." Journal of Holistic Health, 1975-76, pp. 28-29.

Leichtman, Robert. "Clairvoyant Diagnosis." Journal of Holistic Health, 1977, p. 41.

"The Marriage of Science and Religion." SCP (Spiritual Counterfeits Project) Journal 2, no. 1 (August 1978): 17.

May, Antoinette. "Meditation for Inmates." *New Realities* 1, no. 3:48.

Neubert, Robert. "Profile: Robert Leichtman, M.D." *Psychic*, January-February 1976, p. 34.

Nelson, Harry. "American Way of Life is Killing Us, Expert Contends," *Los Angeles Times*, 3 April 1978, part 2, p. 1.

New Realities (Psychic) magazine, 1970-79.

North, Gary K. "Economic Commentary: Magic, Envy, and Economic Underdevelopments." *Journal of Christian Reconstruction*, Symposium on Satanism, 2 (Winter 1974): 149-62.

Psychic (New Realities) April 1972; August 1975, p. 50.

Science of Mind, February 1979.

SCP (Spiritual Counterfeits Project) Journal 2, no. 1 (August 1978): 17.

"Shafika Karagulla: Interview." *Psychic*, August 1973, p. 10.

Shealy, C. Norman. "Perspectives on Psychic Diagnosis." *ARE Journal*, September 1976, pp. 208-9.

Simon, Allie; Worthen, David M.; and Mitas, John A. II." An Evaluation of Iridology."*Journal of the American Medical Association*, 242, no. 13 (28 September 1979): 1385.

Synthesis. Journal of the Psychosynthesis Institutes of the Synthesis Graduate School for the Study of Man, San Francisco, London, and Rotterdam, 2d rev. ed., 1978.

Theta Magazine. Journal of the Psychical Research Foundation, Durham, N.C., 1972-79.

Unger, Merrill F. "Divine Healing." *Bibliotheca Sacra*, July-September 1971, p. 242.

Yoga Journal. September-October 1976, pp. 18-20.

OTHER SOURCES

American Spiritual Healing Association Member-
ship Brochure. Framingham, Mass.: American
Spiritual Healing Association, 1977.
Association for Research and Enlightenment Cir-
culating Files,: Virginia Beach, Va.: ARE
Christ Consciousness
Heaven and Hell
Jesus the Christ, Second Coming.
Jesus, the Pattern and You
The Occult
Oneness of Life and Death
Planetary Sojourns and Astrology
Reincarnation, Part 1
Sin
Spiritual Advice
Truth
Nimoy, Leonard. "In Search of Witchdoctors." Aired
15 April 1978 on KNBC-TV San Diego.

INDEX

Abrams, Albert, and "Black Box," 55
Academy of Parapsychology and Medicine
  and Edgar Cayce, 69
  and occultism, 17
Akashic records, 98, 156
Association for Research and Enlightenment (ARE)
  and Edgar Cayce, 19
  and occultism, 19, 68-69
Association for the Understanding of Man
  and mediumism, 31
Astrology, and medicine/occultism, 41-42
Biblical doctrine, importance of, 212-13
Biblical healing
  Christian errors in, 209-31
  versus occult healing, 106-7, 142, 175-76, 197-202
Bradley, Robert, M.D.
  Bradley method of natural childbirth, 17
  and mediumism, 17
Cayce, Edgar
  and Christianity, 70-76
  and Satan, 72
  and spiritism, 66, 79
"Course in Miracles," spirit-written, 20
Cure rates, 158-60, 166-76, 194-95

De La Warr, George, and spiritism, 58
Edwards, Harry, and spiritism, 99-100, 201
Effectiveness of psychic healing, 15-16. See also
    Cures
Faith healing, 218-26
Fatima (Portugal), 108-9
Fraud, 115, 163-66
God, redefined as occult power, 94, 96, 156-57. See
    also Occult, examples of redefining
Healing
    Christian errors in, 209-31
    and degree of faith, 218-28
    methodology irrelevant in psychic (as contrasted
        to conventional) healing, 54-56, 60-62, 93
Healing in the atonement theory, 215-18
Healing shrines, 107-10
Holistic health
    and occult, 19, 43
    treatments, 18, 27
    unbiblical aspects of, 67, 76, 78
Hypnosis, and mesmerism, 37-39
Implications of new psycho-spiritual disciplines,
    9-11, 14
Institute for Noetic Sciences, 18, 52
Jampolsky, Gerald, and spiritism, 20
Kreiger, Dolores, and psychic healing, 22
Kubler-Ross, Elizabeth, and spiritism, 20-21
Leichtman, Robert, M.D., example of holistic health
    trend, 42-46
LeShan, Lawrence, 100-4
Lourdes (France), occultic/unbiblical impact, 108-9
Medicine
    and Edgar Cayce, 68, 78
    and occultism historically, 18, 41-43
Mediumism/spiritism
    in hospitals, 15, 20
    and professionals, 20-22

Mesmerism (animal magnetism), 35-39
  and hypnotism, 37-38
  and mediumism, 36-39
Mind power, 156, 209-10, 213-15, 218
Mitchell, Edgar, supporter of psychic healing, 15
Monism, and spiritual warfare, 156
Montgomery, Ruth (medium), 97
"Mr. A," 96-99
Occult
  energy, 103-4
  examples of redefining, 19, 25-26, 43, 45-46, 56,
    60, 80, 88, 93, 95, 141-43, 153-58, 206
  hazards of, 9-10, 48, 59, 65, 71, 90-91, 97, 100,
    102-5, 125, 160-61, 174-75, 191-99
  idolatry, 192-93
  immorality of, 80-84
  powers-acquisition, 197
Oyle, Irving, and spiritism, 20
Parapsychology, 9-10, 35, 93, 168-69, 191-92, 202-5,
    233
Peterson, Ross, and spiritism, 80
Positive confession/thinking, 209-10, 213-15, 218
Psychic diagnosis
  common elements of, 32-33
  defined, 14, 29-30
  and mesmerism/hypnotism, 33-40
  occult history of, 33-39
  and occult revivals, 33-34
  by pendulum, 31-32
  and physicians, 29
  in psychic surgery, 120
  reality of, 30-33
  and spiritism, 30, 136
  success of, 40
  supernatural rather than natural ability, 29-30,
    32-33

Psychic healing
  ability uncontrollable, 32, 96, 125, 152
  versus conventional treatment, 16
  cures, 158-60
  dangers of, 81, 125, 160-61, 191-99
  defined, 14-16
  developed by occult methods, 157
  and faith, 176-80, 194-95, 206-7
  and healers, 88, 91-105
  healers as mediums, 158
  and healers' philosophy, 184-87
  historic roots of, 18, 22
  impact of, 15-22, 153
  methodology peripheral, 93, 159, 170. See also
    Radionics
  and monism, 156
  not an innate power, 89-90, 92, 94, 98-99, 114, 154,
    156, 163, 178, 185, 201, 234-35
  and physicians, 17-22
  and psychic diagnosis, 87
  purpose of, 206-7
  redefined, 88
  social implications of, 22-26, 76-78, 120, 161-63,
    168-70, 174, 180-84
  spirits not always sensed, 105, 107
  and spiritism, 88-90, 106, 154
  spiritistic hypothesis on, unity, 88-90, 149-50,
    157-58, 201-2
  and spirit selection, 139
  and trance, 140
  and witchcraft, 16-17
Psychic surgery
  and altered consciousness, 140-42
  apported phenomena, 131-33, 158, 166-67
  dangers of, 175
  defined, 15
  and diagnosis, 120

false or temporary cures, 130, 132
forms of, 114
hostility to medical surgery and conditions, 115-16, 134-35
and mediumism, 114, 136
not innate power, 114
ruthless methods, 118-19, 129-30, 134
and Sai Baba, 23
and shamanism, 135-39
and spirit accommodation, 142-46
and spirit selection, 139
the surgeons, 116-30
Psychometry
defined, 14, 30, 54
radionics a form of, 54, 60-62
psychic, not scientific, 56, 58-62
spiritistic, 58-62
Radionics
devices peripheral to psychic power, 54-56, 60-62, 170
and psychometry, 54, 60-62
Reincarnation, and abortions, 83
Sai Baba, and psychic surgery, 23
Semantics, and spiritual warfare, 153-58. See also Occult, examples of redefining
Spiritism
source of psychic healing, 88-90, 106, 87-110, 114, 154
unbiblical revelations, 50
Stanford, Ray and Rex, and spiritism, 31
Thunder, Rolling, and spiritism, 91-93
Wallace, Amy, The Psychic Healing Book, 16
Water dowsing
and psychic activity, 55
and psychometry, 53
Worrall, Olga and Ambrose, and spiritism, 93-96